NATURAL MAGIC

NATURAL MAGIC

Craft spells in alignment with nature and
the magical world

Marie Bruce

SIRIUS

All images courtesy of Shutterstock

SIRIUS

This edition published in 2024 by Sirius Publishing, a division of
Arcturus Publishing Limited,
26/27 Bickels Yard, 151–153 Bermondsey Street,
London SE1 3HA

ISBN: 978-1-3988-4493-3
AD012160UK

Printed in China

CONTENTS

INTRODUCTION

Follow the mossy stepping-stones...

Have you ever felt a sense of enchantment as you wander around a woodland, or sink into the grass in a park or garden on a hot summer day, content to watch the clouds race and the trees sway? Have you ever stirred a simple cup of herbal tea with a wish in your heart and then imagined that wish coming true as you sipped the brew? Or perhaps you feel a strong affinity with birds and wildlife, convinced that they have something to tell you, some wise message to pass on? If so, it could be that you are a natural witch, or a green witch.

The magic of the natural witch has often been depicted in folklore and she is a staple character in many fables. She is frequently shown living in a cottage at the edge of a dense forest, where she forages for food, remedies, and supplies for the spells she casts over a bonfire, in her tangled garden of herbs and flowers. She is sometimes old, sometimes young, usually living alone or with sister witches, but she is always powerful. She lives in tune with the world around her, a student of the earth, studying the lore of plants. She is both a guardian and protector of her environment, giving and receiving magical energy to work her will.

Such is the stereotype, yet the modern-day natural witch is just as likely to be found living in a large city, foraging herbs from her windowsill or balcony, as she is to be living a rural life in the countryside. She might not be a woman at all, as more and more men are also finding the green path, so although I use the feminine pronoun throughout this book, it is of course a non-binary practice and natural magic is for everyone who is drawn to nature. It is for all those who find their soul stirred by the quickening of the earth and who feel most at ease when they are in a green space, be that a garden, a park, a room full of house-plants or the dark forests of the fairy tale. Natural magic is a mossy labyrinth of stepping stones, designed to lead its practitioners right back into the ancient realm of forest lore, straight to the heart of Mother Earth, so tread lightly, for she feels your presence. Step into my secret garden of magic and enchantment, as you learn to see with glimmering green eyes.

Serene blessings,
Marie Bruce x

FOLLOW THE MOSSY STEPPING-STONES ...

7

PART

1

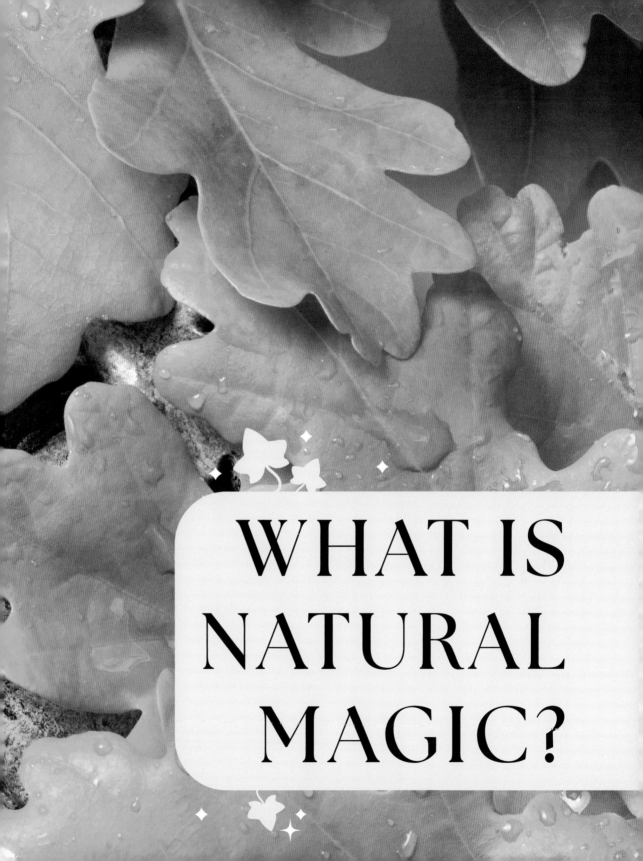

WHAT IS
NATURAL
MAGIC?

As an earth-based spirituality, witchcraft is intrinsically linked to nature and the environment. While all witches work with the earth's power in some capacity, natural witches dedicate their entire practice to the magic and lore of plants, trees, herbs and flowers. They immerse themselves in the natural world around them, taking great joy in the tiniest bud that pushes between the pave-stones of a city street, or spending time with a favourite tree as if it were an old friend. These witches feel the life force of plants very acutely, nurturing and caring for them like children, using them in spells, rituals and healing remedies. It is a much simpler practice than Wicca, which is high ceremonial magic, and the natural witch works predominantly alone, from her own home and natural surroundings. Also known as a hedge witch or green witch, she is a combination of environmentalist, activist, herbalist, healer, charmer, and devotee to wildlife. So how do you know if you are one yourself? Look out for the signs listed opposite.

Signs you might be drawn to natural magic

◇ You feel energized when out in nature
◇ Green spaces make you happy and uplifted
◇ You are inclined to grow plants and herbs
◇ You enjoy gardening
◇ Even in a small space, you bring nature in with potted plants and crystals
◇ You prefer the great outdoors and spend as much time outside as you can
◇ You are intrigued by the many benefits of plants and their healing properties
◇ You create 'gardens' wherever you can, on windowsills, in corridors, on balconies etc.
◇ You feel an affinity with wildlife and chat to the birds, bees and wild creatures you meet
◇ You feel saddened by environmental issues such as global warming
◇ The moon attracts you each and every night

If any of this seems familiar, then it is likely that you have an innate aptitude for natural magic. This book will help you to hone those skills into a positive practice.

Guardians of the Green

Followers of the natural magic path often see themselves as the guardians of the environment. They take their responsibility to the earth very seriously and will campaign against the felling of healthy trees, deforestation, pollution, global warming and so on. At the same time, they are usually active in their community, looking for ways to create or care for green spaces, clearing litter, raising awareness of local environmental issues and doing what they can to ensure that the world remains green and growing, healthy and abundant.

In this sense natural witches work on both a micro and macro-cosmic scale. Her microcosm is her own space, her home and garden. It is here that the bulk of her work is carried out, growing, harvesting and using herbs, casting spells and rituals, and so on. Natural witches tend to their own environment with all due diligence, ensuring that they mitigate any negative impact on the Earth. This might mean that they recycle, reuse and shop second-hand. It could also include a vegan or vegetarian diet, using natural cleaning products for housework, and so on. Natural witches try to live as ethically as possible, being mindful of the impact their daily habits and routines have on the environment.

At the same time, they will also work with the macrocosm of their immediate community and the world at large, supporting global issues such as sustainable energy, rewilding projects, equality, human and animal rights. In this way, natural witches become activists, raising their voices to have a positive influence and impact on the policies and politics of the time, because when you feel a close connection to the earth, you want to protect and defend it. In recent years, as we come to see the devastating effects of global warming, this activist activity has become more ingrained into the practice of natural magic.

Notable Natural Magic Practitioners

Some natural witches have been very outspoken about their wish to protect the earth, carrying the ideology of natural magic into the mainstream by publishing books, appearing on TV, offering workshops and being key speakers at events and seminars. Here are some of the most notable natural or green witches of today.

Starhawk

When American feminist, Starhawk, first published her book *The Spiral Dance* in 1979, she could not possibly have known that she was beginning a movement, but the Goddess Movement, as it is called, has been a popular path for many pagans to follow, providing a guiding light ever since. She has been very vocal about her belief in the Earth as a living being, one which we all have a duty to care for and protect. Discover more at Starhawk.org

Glennie Kindred

As a British artist and writer, Glennie Kindred has a reputation for exploring the sacred meaning in her native landscape and her place within it. She brings her love of nature to the page, both writing and illustrating her beautiful books, which are full of herb lore, sacred sites and self-empowerment achieved via a spiritual connection with the Earth. She gives talks and workshops to help people reconnect with the environment in a spiritual way. Find her at glenniekindred.co.uk

Emma Restall Orr

A British Druid, Emma Restall Orr has walked the pagan path for many years and she is a well-known figure of the pagan community, frequently appearing at the Witchfest festival and at sacred sites such as Stonehenge. She has written several books on her green practice, including introductions for beginners, as well as personal memoirs of her life as a Druid Priestess. In writing such books, she has effectively documented druidry, which is more commonly seen as an oral tradition, thus helping those who seek a greener path to find their way more easily through her written guidance.

The Witch Wound

In the past, both witches and druids were persecuted for their beliefs and were often executed. In England and America, witches were hanged; in Europe they were burnt at the stake, while in Scotland they were either burnt at the stake or burnt in a barrel. Interestingly, Wales didn't succumb to the witch-craze and only a handful of so-called witches were ever executed there. What did the Welsh see that the rest of Britain, Europe and America failed to register?!

It is also interesting that many of the *accusers* were also women – neighbours, former friends, love rivals and sometimes even relatives of the accused. These women were often acting from spite or envy, bearing a grudge and pointing the finger to exact revenge for some kind of perceived slight or wrong-doing. After all, what better way to get rid of your husband's lover than by accusing her of witchcraft, thereby sending her straight to the stake! Problem solved! Women set against women – we call this *female relational aggression* and, along with social cleansing, it was one of the driving forces behind the witch trials.

The witch-craze lasted from the 14th to the 17th century and many lives were lost because of it. This historical or hereditary trauma is still occasionally felt by modern witches and we call it the Witch Wound. It is experienced as a feeling of uneasiness when faced with certain places or types of magic. It can even lead to a reluctance to experience any degree of power at all, both personally and professionally. It is especially likely to be felt when visiting a place where witches were held, tortured or executed, so castle dungeons or known execution sites. Places such as Lancaster Castle, where the Pendle Witches were held prior to execution, or the Witch's Stone in Dornoch, where the last witch-burning in Scotland was held in 1727, executing the accused witch, Janet Horne, are highly likely to trigger the uneasiness of the Witch Wound, depending on how sensitive you are to such energies.

In recent times, there have been attempts to heal this ancient Witch Wound, by honouring the lives of those accused. Scotland seems to be leading the way with this, as the First Minister of Scotland, Nicola Sturgeon, offered a formal apology to all those accused and executed of witchcraft in Scotland during the witch hunts. She made this formal apology on International Women's Day. Hopefully, other countries will soon follow suit.

Tools and Attire

Before you begin your foray into the realms of natural magic, it is a good idea to try and collect the following tools, which will help you in your rituals and protect you in your rambles through the wildwood. You don't need to spend a lot of money or gather them all at once. As you will see, many of these tools are common household items, others can be hand-made or found in thrift shops.

◇ Waterproof boots – to keep your feet dry when trudging through muddy forests

◇ Basket – to collect foraged items or carry ritual materials outside

◇ Green Witch Cloak – to offer warmth and camouflage, allowing wildlife to come closer and make friends with you

◇ Botanical books/apps – to check and double check species and identifications

◇ Notebooks – to record your travels, spells, rituals, profile herbs and so on

- Secateurs, small scythe or boline – to harvest herbs, berries, blossom etc.
- Mortar and pestle – to grind dried herbs for spells
- Cauldron – to hold items, burn fire spells, or hold water for divination
- Gardening gloves – to protect your hands from thorny plants who like to bite back!
- Altar Pentacle – to charge your herbs, crystals etc. with magical energy
- Chalice – to hold ritual wine and home-made potions
- Consumables – everything you need to make your magic fly! Spell jars, pouches, string, candles, crystals, essential oils, and so on
- A Green Space – this could be a garden, balcony, local park or woodland

PLANTS – the very essence of natural magic; you won't get very far without their help!

And on we go, to the next mossy stepping-stone…

PART
2

NATURAL MAGIC PANTRY

Step into the natural witch's pantry and you will find a plethora of herbs and flowers, all lined up in jars on a shelf, or drying from a rack and strewn across doorways and windowsills for various protection spells and rituals. In the past, such pantries were also known as *still rooms*, which was an area of a castle in which the lady of the manor, or the chatelaine, would concoct remedies, soaps, candles, cordials and tisanes, for the good of all those who lived beneath her roof. It was an important job and one which the chatelaine would have learnt from her mother and grandmother as a child, in preparation for her future marriage. It could also be a dangerous task, especially during the rise of the witch-craze, as any mistakes could lead to accusations of witchcraft or poisoning.

The 16th-century Queen of France, Catherine de Medici, was well known for dabbling in herbs, potions and lethal poisons, as well as spellcraft. One can only imagine the things that might have been conjured in *her* still room, which was purported to have hundreds of secret compartments hidden in the panelled walls, thought to house her collection of poisons. You wouldn't want to take tea with *her*!

The modern witch's pantry or still room, is much more mundane and it needn't be a room at all. Your witch's pantry could be a cupboard in the kitchen, a dresser, a bookcase, a wooden chest or a set of shelves hung on the wall. Whatever you choose will be determined by your space and budget, but it is here that you will be keeping your jars of dried herbs and spices, essential oils, spell jars, pouches and candles, incense, smudge bundles and crystals. Use whatever space or cabinet appeals to you, or whatever you have to hand. There is no need to buy a new item of furniture – you could perhaps simply clear out a drawer and use that as your witch's pantry. Use your imagination and find a space to house your natural magic supplies. Keep your tools, such as pentacle, mortar and pestle etc. close by so that you have everything to hand when you need it.

23

Mother Earth

Natural Magic is part of the pagan path, which means that all natural witches believe that the Earth is a sacred entity in its own right. We see the Earth as our mother, for we could not survive without her nurturing, nourishing and abundant provision. We live off her generosity in the crops that we eat and the food that we grow. Most natural witches believe in sustainable and responsible farming, turning away from produce that has been flown across the world and choosing to buy locally grown produce instead, or to grow what they can themselves.

Viewed as an aspect of the Divine Feminine, the Earth is honoured and is frequently known as Mother Earth, Gaia or Mother Nature. We are her protectors and collaborators, working with the cycles of the moon and the seasons to nurture our own green spaces. Pollution, consumerism, deforestation and so on, are having a negative impact on the Earth, so we are essentially biting the hand that feeds us. If we do not care for our planet with sustainable living, Earth cannot continue to sustain and care for us indefinitely. Our daily habits need to become eco-friendlier if we are to reverse the damage that has already been done to the planet by industrialisation and consumerism.

Herbalism

Growing, tending, drying and using herbs in spellcraft is the main business of the natural witch. She grows her own spell ingredients as much as possible, forages for what she can, shares and trades supplies with like-minded friends and generally gets her hands dirty! She is never happier than when rambling through the woods hunting for mushrooms, or knee-deep in the garden transplanting seedlings into beds and tucking them in with care. She loves the scent of the earth, the feel of the soil between her fingertips, the softness of new shoots and leaves coming up. Her soul runs as green as the earth after a spring shower and cultivating herbs, plants, flowers and trees puts her in her element.

In its purest form, natural magic does involve growing things, but if you don't have particularly green fingers, you can forage from a friend's garden or use dried herbs from the supermarket if needs be, although if you want to be authentic to the natural magic way, you should really grow your own plants, even if it's only a couple of pots on a windowsill. We will be looking at how to create both indoor and outdoor gardens in the next chapter. For now, suffice to say, that getting acquainted with fresh herbs, flowers and plants is something that most green witches spend their time doing. While a full botany of herbs is somewhat beyond the scope of this book, here are a few of the most magical herbs and plants used by witches.

Angelica
Also known as Masterwort, angelica is a good plant for protection rituals and can help ward away evil energies.

Aloe
Great for treating minor burns, heat rash and skin irritations. Aloe can also be used in beauty potions and treatments to beautify the complexion.

Basil
Basil is a good power booster for spells and is great for protection magic.

Bay
The prosperity herb! Growing bay is said to bring wealth and good fortune. Plant it near your front door to bring prosperity to your home.

Broom
A magical shrub that has literally been used to make brooms or besoms for centuries. Great for cleansing rituals and protection of boundaries.

Burdock
Thought to guard against negative energies, ill-wishing and bad vibes, burdock has purification and protective properties.

Chamomile
A herb of rest, relaxation, anti-stress and soothing sleep. Great for night time teas, healing tisanes and moments of peaceful meditation.

Catnip
This little herb sends felines nuts! They love it because it gives them a natural feeling of euphoria. A great one to grow if you have feline familiars.

Cinnamon
Ground cinnamon is commonly added to prosperity and abundance spells. It is also nice in teas as it has a warming and soothing effect.

Clover
A magical little plant said to bring good luck, so it is often used in spells to reverse a period of bad luck or to bring about a lucky break of some kind.

Clove
Clove is used to stop gossip, slander, sabotage and back-stabbing. It is also a well known cure for toothache.

Dandelion
Much maligned as a common weed, the humble dandelion can be used in spells for transformation, ambition and recognition. Steeped as a tea it is a great aid to the digestive system.

Elder
Both the fruit and the flowers of the elder tree are beneficial and can be used in cooking and when brewing cordials and wines. In spellcraft, elder is used to define and protect boundaries and also to connect with the Crone Goddess or Elder Mother.

Eucalyptus
Great for steam baths to ease congestion and can also be dried and burnt to clear obstacles from your path. Good to add to smudge bundles.

Fennel
The seeds can be added to spell pouches for protection and purification. The plant can also be hung over thresholds to protect boundaries.

Fern

These represent the slow unfolding of events. Magically they represent love, protection and patience.

Geranium

A pretty plant which signifies love, especially self-love. Geranium tea is very good for easing menstrual cramps and tensions.

Gorse

A prickly shrub that can bloom with golden flowers throughout the year. Best planted by garden gates, paths and doors to ward away unwelcome visitors.

Hyssop

A lovely plant that attracts all kinds of wildlife, from birds and bees to butterflies and moths. Hyssop is a staple in the cottage garden and great in borders. Magically it can be used to attune with the fey, the earth and wildlife.

Hawthorn

May blossom is said to hold the spirit of the spring goddess and so this tree is honoured on May Day.

Traditionally it is one of the fairy triad trees of oak, ash and thorn, and where these three grow together, fairy activity is present.

Holly

Represents the green man in his aspect as Holly King, the ruler of the dark season. Holly is great for protection and is traditionally viewed as the Yule plant.

Ivy

Magically, ivy can be used in binding spells, to keep someone from acting against you or to keep secrets. Also represents the green woman or wode wives.

Jasmine

Jasmine can be used to create lovely bath potions and beauty treatments. It is thought to bring love to one who wears it.

Juniper

Lends protection from unforeseen events and accidents. Juniper is also said to attract love and positive attention, plus if placed by the door, it will guard against thieves and intruders.

Lavender

A fantastic all-rounder. Lavender is good for all kinds of magic, predominantly love, protection, purification, healing and sleep. If you grow nothing else, cultivate some lavender!

Mint

Powerful herb for prosperity, abundance, wealth, money, savings, ambition and career progression. Also known for its uplifting and refreshing properties.

Mugwort

A traditional witches herb, mugwort is often used to reduce swelling, bruising and to treat mild tummy upsets. Magically it is regarded as one of the wise woman's herbs as it was used to bring on visions, prophetic dreams and clairvoyance. At the same time, it was often given to women to bring on menstruation.

Nettle

Most often used in spells to stop gossip and spite, nettles can be added to spells to make someone feel the sting of their own words.

Patchouli

A great herb for prosperity, protection, love, passion and romance, so why wouldn't you want some patchouli in your life?

Rowan

The berries and bark are used in protection charms and spells.

Sage

Sage is the purification herb and it is frequently made into bundles and burnt in ritual cleansings. These bundles are called smudge sticks and you can easily make them yourself at home (see page 31). It is good for healing, particularly healing a rift between two parties. It can also be added to protection and prosperity magic.

Thyme

Another herb that is said to aid in psychic visions, divinations and prophecy.

Valerian

Great to aid restful sleep or to bring about dreams of a future lover.

Vervain

A good protection herb, particularly useful when the danger is ever-present, so for the protection of the armed forces and emergency services for example.

Wormwood

Also known as the Green Fairy, wormwood is said to bring about visions, inspiration and a feeling of euphoria. When steeped in alcohol it becomes the Poet's Draught, or absinthe, beloved of the great Romantic Poets such as Lord Byron and Percy Bysshe Shelley. These days it is more commonly sold as absinthe!

Yarrow

Yarrow can be used to break a fever, bring down a temperature and ease digestive complaints. When drunk as a tea, it can help to boost immunity and ward off seasonal colds and flu, plus it is said to be a good cure for a hangover.

These are just some of the plants used by witches in their magic and this list is by no means exhaustive. Feel free to do your own research into the herbs, plants and flowers that are native to your own area and their magical and medicinal uses. Be sure to use a good botanical when trying to identify plants in the wild and remember, there are no such things as *weeds*, there are only *wild flowers*.

How to Make an Herb Drying Rack

Items required:
- ◇ *five twigs or sticks*
- ◇ *a ball of twine*
- ◇ *metal shower hooks*
- ◇ coloured ribbon (optional)

Are you ready to start foraging for magical items? If so, go out into the forest, your garden or a local park on a windy day. Find a place with many trees and stand beneath them. Close your eyes and silently ask the tree spirits to guide you to the best naturally shed twigs. Gather five twigs, each about 30cm in length and 2–5cm thick. Take them home, giving thanks to the trees and place the twigs to dry out thoroughly. Once dry, lay the twigs in the shape of a pentacle or five pointed star and secure each point with string. Add equal lengths of string or pretty ribbon from both ends of the star so that you can hang it up in a horizontal position, to create a rack. Next, place the shower hooks around the pentacle, ready to hold bunches of herbs and flowers upside down to dry. Finally, find a space in your home to hang the drying rack, which would traditionally be placed in the kitchen, still room or conservatory.

Sage and Lavender Smudge Bundles

Items required:
◇ *enough fresh sage and lavender to create a couple of bundles*
◇ *natural twine or string*

To make your own smudge bundles, harvest enough fresh stems of sage and lavender to make two bundles, each approximately 5cm in diameter. Begin with the sage and make it into a small posy in your hand, adding a stem at a time, then adding stems of lavender on top. Make sure the bundle is as even as possible, then holding it firmly, begin to wrap the string around the bundle, moving from the stems of the herbs to the top and back again so that the string criss-crosses and secures the herbs in place. Tie the string tightly to secure the bundle and hang upside down from your drying rack. Leave in place until all the herbs have dried thoroughly, right the way through. To use, light the end of the smudge bundle until it glows red, then blow out the flame and allow the bundle to smoulder. Gently waft the fragrant smoke around yourself, your home and property, to cleanse the area of all negative energy and bad vibes. When you have finished, stub out the bundle and leave it in an ashtray until you are sure it has been extinguished. Repeat each month as the moon wanes, to keep your space positive and peaceful.

PART
3

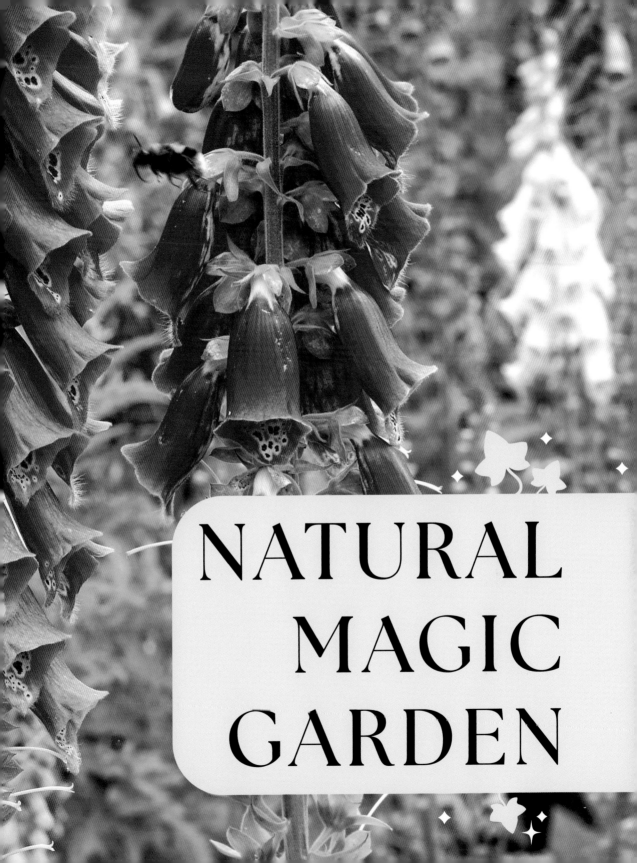

NATURAL
MAGIC
GARDEN

Natural Magic is all about communing with the earth, getting outside and enjoying the nature which gives the practice its name. It is essential that you have a green space or garden of your own, but do not worry if you don't have an outside space, as you can create an indoor garden which is just as magical. Attuning with plants and trees is good for the soul. It decreases stress levels and lowers blood pressure. The fresh air fills the lungs as plants naturally help with pollution by purifying the air around them. So there are many benefits to nurturing a garden of your own.

The Nemeton Grove

In Celtic and Druidic culture, the nemeton grove was a sacred outdoor space where special gatherings, rituals and celebrations would be held. It was similar to an outdoor church, with rituals and important decisions being held and made in the nemeton, for the good of the whole clan. The natural witch's garden is her own kind of nemeton grove, for she tends to it as the sacred space it is. It is here that the natural witch grows ingredients for spells and potions, where she studies herbs and their properties and where she interacts with the wildlife, actively encouraging birds, bees, foxes, hares and so on to visit her garden. The witch's nemeton grove is likely to have a special seating area, perhaps a table for potting seedlings or writing herb profiles in notebooks, a water feature of some kind, be this a simple bird bath or an elaborate pond, and lots of feeders and habitats for wildlife to thrive. The witch's garden is always a hive of activity, even in the winter time as birds come to rely on the food she provides to see them through the colder months.

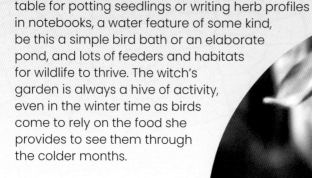

Creating an Outdoor Garden

If you have an outdoor space, you can create a beautiful witch's garden and nemeton grove of your own. Designing and nurturing a garden is a long term commitment, but it is something that brings joy to many people. Think beyond regimental rows of flower beds and try to craft something that has wildness at its heart. Your garden should reflect your interests in natural magic and it doesn't matter if your neighbours do not approve of you ripping out a brick barbecue so that you can build a medicinal herb garden instead. It is your space to use as you wish, so plants herbs, flowers, shrubs and trees to your heart's content.

Take inspiration from the cloister gardens of old convents and monasteries, if you want to see what a useful magical garden looks like. Visit stately homes for inspiration and recreate your favourite aspects of their grounds on a smaller scale. Try to create a garden that appeals to all of your senses, so plant flowers for colour and fragrance, add different levels and different size shrubs to appeal to the eye, include both evergreen and variegated foliage, plant herbs for flavour and texture, add chimes and feeders to fill the space with sound and so on. Make the space as magical as you can, but don't forget to leave a little corner of your garden quite wild in order to encourage the fey folk! Remember that any garden takes time to mature and grow, so you are not going to have a witch's garden overnight, but you can start with whatever you have, be that potted herbs from the supermarket, or cuttings from your neighbours. Make a start and enjoy the process, because there is nothing more charming than picking chamomile flowers from your own garden to brew into a soothing cup of tea.

Creating an Indoor Garden

What if you don't have an outside space of your own? Can you still do natural magic if you don't even have a balcony? Of course you can! There are many plants that thrive indoors so house plants are your best friends. In fact, most natural witches do not confine their foliage friends just to the outdoors, they tend to have indoors spaces full of greenery too. Cacti, miniature rose trees, crocuses, ferns, basil, lemon balm, mint etc., will all do well in pots, so visit the local garden centre and see what appeals to you in their house plant section.

All the same rules apply for an indoor garden as for the outdoor one, so create a collection of potted plants in your home which stimulates all the senses. Have flowering plants for colour, herbs on the windowsill for flavour, use hanging baskets, plant stands and shelving to create different levels of greenery and to add interest. You can even add a bird feeder and a suction bath to the outside of a window to encourage your feathered friends to come along for dinner and a splash around, so that you can enjoy the melody of their frolicking and singing. Nestle crystals in among the foliage for added sparkle and hang a green man plaque on the wall to honour the spirit of the greenwood. Surround yourself with the nature that you love and even if you live in a high rise apartment, you will soon feel that you have an enchanted garden of your own that you can't wait to come home to, living your best natural magic life.

Gardening by the Moon

Witches observe the cycles of the moon and our magic is cast in accordance with the lunar cycle. Natural magic is no different, and just as the moon has a gravitational pull on the tides of the ocean, so too does this pull affect the growth of plants. With this in mind, most witches tend to garden in accordance with the phase of the moon, as follows.

Dark Moon – This is traditionally a time of rest, just before the new moon appears in the sky, so it's the best time to read gardening magazines and books on green witchcraft, to catalogue seeds and so on.

New Moon – great for making plans, designing flower beds and plotting garden improvements on paper, or collecting seeds ready for planting. Also a good time to plant leafy plants such as ferns, shrubs and trees.

Waxing Moon – as the moon grows from new to full, this is the time to plant new seeds, put your garden plans into action and move seedlings outdoors. Great for planting anything which bears berries or fruit.

Full Moon – the best time to repot plants that need more space, to move plants from one area of the garden to another, to harvest fruit, berries and herbs or to cut flowers for the house.

Waning Moon – As the moon wanes and the light diminishes, now is a good time to tend to the soil, to feed the roots and offer libations (traditionally called wassailing) or to plant root crops such as carrots and parsnips. This is also a good time to plant a new crop of bulbs that you want to flourish the following year, so bluebells, daffodils and on so. Deadheading, pruning and tree lopping should also be done during a waning moon.

In addition to following the lunar cycle, green witches also work in accordance with the seasons in general when it comes to maintaining their gardens.

Spring – sowing seeds and young plants, moving seedlings outdoors

Summer – feeding plants and cultivating beds, weeding, maintaining lawns and hedgerows

Autumn – harvesting, clearing leaves, bringing vulnerable plants indoors, preparing for winter by strengthening boundaries and fences

Winter – feeding wildlife, de-icing ponds and water features, pruning and lopping

Invoke a Guardian for your Garden

Items required:
- ◆ a garden lantern and candle or tea light
- ◆ a fairy sun-catcher

Moon Phase:
- ◆ full moon

Once you have created your garden, you might like to invoke a guardian to watch over it. Witches see the life force in everything, which means that each plant has its own spirit. Overall, the fey or faerie folk, are said to be the guardians of the natural world, including gardens, parks and woodlands. You can invoke a fey guardian for your space in the following way. To begin with, light a tea-light and place it in a lantern that is suitable for outdoors and carry this to your garden, along with the sun-catcher. Place them both on the floor or a table and breathe deeply three times. Close your eyes and say:

Guardian of this space, fey spirit of my dreaming

I ask that you protect this place, this realm of growth and greening

Help me to create a sacred grove of peace

A spiritual retreat beneath enchanted trees

Guard and guide me as I tend our garden with care

Impart your shining wisdom in this place and leave it there

So mote it be

Find a place to keep the lantern and hang the sun-catcher where it will bounce the light around the garden. Spend as much time in your nemeton grove as you can and enjoy the space you have conjured.

PART
4

GREEN FOLKLORE

Do you know what to do if you are being pixie-led, or what time of year is the most auspicious for asking the Green Man for a boon? Natural magic is naturally steeped in fey folklore, because you are working with the forest and plants which the fey spirits protect. Many natural witches like to work faerie craft too, communing with the nature spirits of flowers, trees and hedgerows as they forage and work their rituals. In this chapter you will learn more about these enchanted beings.

The Green Man and Wood Wose

The Green Man is the spirit of foliage and trees. Made of leaves and bark, root and branch, he is present in every shrub, plant and tree. Also known as a Wood Wose, he is the guardian of the forest, sometimes referred to as the Lord of the Wildwood. Look closely and you will see his face in the bark. Look up and you are likely to see him carved into the vaults of churches, or spouting rain water from castles and old universities and other buildings. He was a popular motif of Medieval architecture, so it is highly likely that he has been watching over you from one vantage point or another at some stage in your life. His presence in old churches signifies the transition from the old pagan ways, to the new Christian religion, as the stone masons would incorporate his face in an act of reverence for the Old Religion, as paganism is sometimes known.

Whenever you are in a woodland or forest, or even in the smallest copse of trees and shrubs, the Green Man is present. He changes with the seasons, his foliage face going from spring green to autumn gold to frosted bark, as the Wheel of the Year turns, but he is ever present. You might feel him as a presence, watching you from behind the leaves. It can be quite a spooky feeling at times, but he is simply guarding his territory, as any good sentry would do. Look out for him next time you are in a wooded area, or in an old church or university building. See if you can see him peering at you from the bark or the stone foliage. Like the Great Goddess, the green man has several aspects and he is known by different names.

Aspects of the Green Man

- **Holly King –** the Green Man of the dark half of the year, coming into power on the autumnal equinox. He presides over the winter months in the forest.

- **Oak King –** Brother to the Holly King, the Oak King presides over the lighter half of the year. He does battle with his bother on the spring equinox and wins, bringing in the spring and summer months. He presides over the forest until the next battle in autumn, when the Holly King wins and takes over once again.

- **John Barleycorn –** the spirit of the harvest, John Barleycorn is the sacrificial god of the crops, laying down his life before the scythe in order to feed the population.

- **Herne the Hunter –** another Lord of the Trees and the Hunt, Herne is closely associated with Windsor Great Park, where he stepped in front of a rampaging stag to protect the King of England. His name has become intertwined with Green Man mythology and folklore. He is viewed as an aspect of the witch's god, along with his older Celtic counterpart, Cernunnos.

- **Jack in the Green/Puck/Robin Hood –** in this aspect, the Green Man becomes the Trickster, playing jokes on travellers, leading them astray, or exacting a price for passing through his realm. This price could be the loss of a piece of jewellery or a coin, or it could be a blood price, in the form of cuts and scratches from thorny plants.

- **Jack Frost –** the Green Man of the winter woods and counterpart to Jack in the Green. As his name suggests, Jack Frost paints the trees with frost and snow, hangs icicles from the branches and turns the forest into a winter wonderland of silver and white.

Ritual to Ask the Green Man for a Boon

Items required:
- ◆ a pretty crystal for an offering

Moon Phase:
- ◆ full moon

Magical tradition states that twice a year you may ask the Green Man for a magical boon. This request should take place at either the summer or winter solstice, when the respective Oak and Holly Kings are at the height of their power. If you want something to come towards you, then beseech the Oak King. If you want to remove something, such as illness, then ask the Holly King to take it away with him when he falls. You can also request seasonal boons from each King, so a lovely summer holiday from the Oak King or a fantastic Yuletide from the Holly King.

The timing of your ritual will depend on what it is you require and which aspect of the Green Man you are invoking, but it should always be cast on the full moon, preferably outdoors under the trees. Take your crystal with you and find a tree that feels friendly and comfortable with your presence. Introduce yourself and state your purpose and intention, asking for the boon you require, then say:

I have a wish that I wish to be seen

I bring it here to the Man in the Green

Oak/Holly King, grant me this boon

And let my request be granted right soon

In love and trust I make this plea

And leave below this gift for thee

Place the crystal at the root of the tree and leave it there when you leave the woods. Your wish should be granted before your chosen Green King's demise, so within three months.

Faces in the Bark Ritual

Items required:
- a large sheet of paper
- charcoal or wax crayons

Moon Phase:
- perform any time

Take your art supplies with you to the forest or park and look for faces in the bark. Once you find the Green Man looking back at you, take a bark rubbing of his image and take this home with you. You can then frame it and use it to decorate your altar or sacred space.

The Green Woman and Wode Wives

The female counterpart to the Green Man is the Green Woman, also known as a Wode Wife. She is the fey creature which connects the masculine energy of the forest with the ancient feminine energy of Mother Earth. Although she is less common in folklore and architecture than the Green Man, she too is ever present in the woods and her energies are usually more gentle and much less spooky. In folklore, the Wode Wife is a skilled herbalist and healer, a green witch, who can appear as a female form made of moss and bark, bank and blossom, although in some legends she takes on human form and appears with long blonde hair, wearing a white dress. In this respect, Tolkien's character, Galadriel, Queen of the Elves in the Lord of the Ring trilogy, is a depiction of a wode wife. As with many of the female fey spirits, wode wives are said to have very long hair, dressed in leaves, berries and blossom. They are said to appreciate offerings of bread and honey.

Aspects of the Green Woman

- **Dryads –** in Greek mythology, the dryads were the female spirits of trees. They could leave their tree for short periods, but must always return. If the tree was cut down in their absence, they would wander as lost spirits without a home. If the tree was cut down while the dryad spirit was within, she too would die.

- **May Queen –** the spirit of the spring goddess, embodied in the white blossom of the Hawthorn tree, which flowers each May. To bring May blossom indoors is bad luck, and you should only cut hawthorn blossom on May's Eve or May Day.

- **Maid Marian –** the counterpart to Robin Hood, Maid Marian is the matriarch of his band of Merry Men. Like many wode wives, she tends to wounds using the healing power of herbs and can vanish into the forest without trace.

- **Elder Mother –** the Crone spirit of the elder tree, the Elder Mother is the wise woman of the forest. It is considered very bad luck to cut or prune an elder tree without the Elder Mother's permission. Burning elder wood was said to bring a year and a day of misfortune. Respect the Elder!

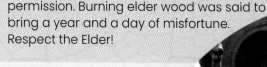

Have You Been Pixie-Led?

Taking a walk or ride in among the trees can be a risky business and it can by easy to lose your way. If you find yourself lost in the woods, having gone round and round in circles, it could be that you have been pixie-led – that is, the forest spirits have been leading you astray! This is something that both the trickster aspects of the Green Man such as Puck or Robin Hood, and the Wode Wives, are thought to do. They use the sounds of the forest, such as falling trees and branches to confuse you and lead you a merry dance. So if you keep hearing the snap of a twig behind you, but no-one is there, it could be that the green spirits of the forest are playing games with you. Tradition states that the best way to end their game, is to turn and wear your coat inside-out to show that you have nothing to hide. That way, you will be led safely back out of the woods.

PART
5

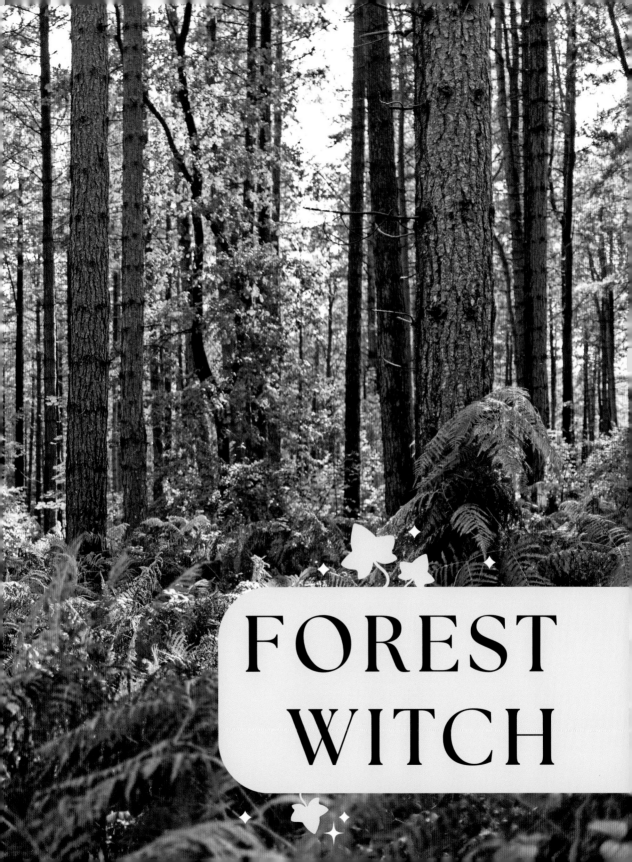

FOREST
WITCH

In medieval times, much of the UK was covered in woodland, which stretched from the south of England, right up to the Caledonian Forest in Scotland. It was called the Great Forest, or the Kingswood, and it was a hive of activity from royal hunting parties chasing deer, to cut-throats and outlaws lying in wait for unwary travellers.

In some areas, small pockets of this forest still remain. One clear indicator of an ancient forest is the presence of English bluebells, so if you live in the UK and you have a small bluebell wood near where you live, chances are it was once a part of the Great Forest. This forest was introduced and ring-fenced by the Normans for their hunting activities, causing much social unrest among the less fortunate, who were forbidden to forage, snare or hunt. To do so was known as *trespassing against the vert and the venison* and it could lead to serious punishment. There are still laws in many woodlands which forbid removing items or picking flowers, so check before you go foraging.

Many witches feel a special affinity with the forest and enjoy spending time in the woods. There is a deep natural magic in any woodland. In all seasons, forests are enchanting places to visit. From the first stirrings of life in spring, to the green-tinged light that fills a summer woodland; from the russet, bronze and gold of autumn leaves to the shimmering frosted evergreens and bare branches of winter, the woodland is always a place of vibrant colour and texture.

A forest is a place of magic and fairy-tale, of spooky shadows and strange sounds. It can be easy to feel unnerved when lost and alone in the woods. Soldiers call this *jungle-fear* and learning how to control it is part of military training. This fear stems, in part, from the separation we now have from the natural world around us. No longer living closely to the rhythm of the land, it can be very easy for a modern city-dweller to feel uneasy in the midst of a forest, but there isn't really anything to be afraid of. The trees can't hurt you and most wildlife will be inclined to avoid you, rather than attack you. That said, there is something rather fun about being spooked in the woods and lots of woodland trusts hold spooky events in the forest during autumn, so check what is happening in your local woods if you want to enjoy a spooky night in the forest. Sherwood Forest holds such spooky events every October, which are great fun. Whichever forest you visit, always be sure to abide by the local rules and laws of that woodland.

The Lungs of the Earth

Forests are a vital part of the natural world and we need them now more than ever. As trees take in carbon dioxide and expel oxygen, they are great air purifiers and can help to combat pollution and global warming. Younger trees take on more carbon dioxide than older ones, which is the logic behind cutting down mature trees and replacing them with saplings. This is thought to help reduce pollution, especially in cities. However, if this continues indefinitely, it means that future generations will not know the thrill of visiting a centuries old tree, such as the Major Oak in Sherwood Forest, so we also need to protect our mature trees as well.

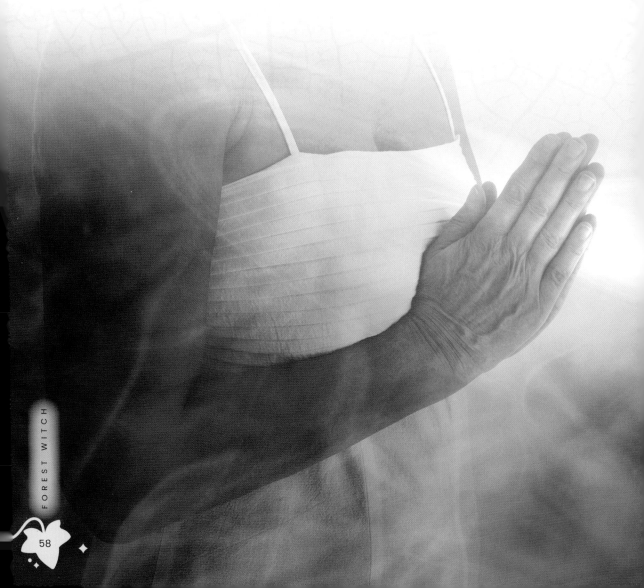

Shared Breathing with Trees

Items required:
◇ a friendly tree

Moon Phase:
◇ perform during a waxing to full moon

Because humans and trees each need what the other expels, shared breathing is a great ritual to perform in a woodland. Go to a place where you can stand or sit comfortably beneath a tree. If you have trees in your garden that would be ideal; if not, visit a park or forest. Get comfortable under the boughs of the tree. Lean against the trunk if you can and tilt your head back to gaze up at the branches stretching out above you. Close your eyes and begin some ritual breathing. Breathe in deeply through your nose for a count of four seconds, hold your breath for four seconds, then breathe out for another four seconds. As you do this visualize your outward breath and carbon dioxide feeding the tree above you, while your inward breath takes in the oxygen that the tree has expelled. Continue sharing breath with the tree in this way for as long as you feel comfortable. The good thing about this exercise is that no-one else knows what you are doing. To anyone who passes by, you are simply sitting beneath a tree in a relaxed and meditative state.

Earth Light

On occasion, if the conditions are right, you might be lucky enough to witness the phenomenon of *earth light* or *living light*. This is when a tree or shrub appears to glow in a green and golden light. The light shimmers all around the tree, looking like a magical portal to another realm, but in fact it is the scientific process known as bioluminescence, which occurs when sunlight hits the chlorophyll which gives plants their green colour. I have witnessed earth light once myself, when I was a young girl and it was an extremely magical experience. It is a beautiful, natural phenomenon, similar to the northern lights and something that you will never forget if you ever see it. Traditionally, earth light was thought to be a portal into the fairy realms and so if you see it, you should make a wish.

The Fairy Triad

Another portal to the fairy realm was the fairy triad, made up of oak, ash and thorn trees. Where these three trees grow together, fairy activity is said to be strongest and it is thought to be a sacred grove. In folklore, it was said that people would be kidnapped by the fey if they walked through the fairy triad, only to return decades later, much older and raving about fairyland. The fairy triad was also said to be a good place to meet a fairy lover, a wode wife or to make a wish, especially if you went there at one of the fairy hours of dawn or dusk. However, you should never leave a baby or child there unattended or the fey might replace them with a changeling. Oak, ash and thorn are all trees that the Druids revered, so they were viewed with disdain by the early Christians, which could explain some of these superstitions.

Foraging

Foraging is about using the gifts of nature in your magic and the forest is full of treasure. It is a fun activity, but foraging should always be conducted with respect. Never take more than you need and ask permission from the spirit of the plant or tree first. Some woodlands have strict rules about foraging and many wild flowers are protected, including bluebells, so you should not pick them. Remember that some woodlands are also privately owned and while the landowners allow the public access, these green spaces should not be foraged without permission from the estate manager.

It goes without saying that you should never dig up plants or remove bulbs from the ground, nor should you scrape lichen etc. from trees. In general, only forage what the wood no longer needs, so forage from the forest floor if looking for twigs and leaves etc. If you are picking berries, make sure that you can identify them correctly so that you don't make dangerous mistakes – for example, hemlock, which is lethal, is sometimes mistaken for the harmless elder, often used in cooking! So be careful and use your common sense. If you don't know what it is, leave it be. Remember that some plants are toxic when touched and even the humble rose carries poison on its thorns, so wear gloves or carry antiseptic cream with you. Opposite are just a few suggestions as to what you might forage and use in your natural magic.

- Fallen leaves, especially in autumn. These make great botanical displays in a Book of Shadows or hung in frames.
- Pine cones, acorns and seed pods are good for all aspects of abundance magic and prosperity spells. They can also be used in fertility magic too.
- Fallen branches can be repurposed as magical wands, staffs and broom handles.
- Fallen twigs can be fashioned into all kinds of altar and wall decorations, from pentagrams to crescent moons.
- Pine needles can be added to homemade incense and burnt on charcoal blocks for prosperity and winter magic.
- Soil from the forest floor is a great way to connect with a distant sacred place when you are back home, so take a small spell jar and fill it with earth from whichever great, sacred forest you visit. Only take a small amount of top soil away with you. You can add a pinch of this to boundary spells and grounding magic.
- Berries make good natural dyes for magical craft projects and, of course, some, such as blackberries, are edible and great in pies and cordials.
- Blossoms such as elderflower make good bath potions and cordials, as well as natural dyes.
- Mushrooms and fungi – be very careful with this one! Many are toxic so these are perhaps safest left alone, though you can always take photos or make sketches for your Book of Shadows.
- Nuts are good for abundance spells and there is great joy in hunting for sweet chestnuts to roast when in season, or horse chestnuts for games with the kids.

Other Forest Witch Tips

There are many ways you can incorporate the woods into your magical practice and if you are lucky enough to live close to a wood or park then you should make the very most of it. Here are a few more suggestions for you to try.

- ◆ Visit the woods at different phases of the moon and notice how it changes, how the wildlife adapts and how the changing light makes everything look slightly different.

- ◆ Forest bathing, which is simply enjoying and taking in the atmosphere of the forest and the greenery. This is good for your witchy soul.

- ◆ Learn to recognize and imitate bird song. Whistle in the woods and see which birds come closer and start singing with you. Learn to caw like a raven, hoot like an owl or coo like a wood pigeon and start a conversation with your feathered friends.

- ◆ Allow wildlife to come to you. Sit or stand still, be very quiet and see who wants to make friends. It could be a stag, a raven, a fox or a squirrel. Just wait and see who introduces themselves and enjoy the interaction. Animals are naturally curious, so it is only a matter of time before someone wants to know who you are and what you are doing in their home!

- ◆ Introduce yourself to the forest. Say hello. Welcome the new buds in spring, thank the leaves as they fall to the ground in autumn. Talk to the spirits of the forest. They've been waiting for you.

- ◆ Remember that no matter where you live, nature is all around you. You just have to look for it and honour it when you find it in order to live magically!

PART

6

THE
LANGUAGE
AND MAGIC
OF FLOWERS

Flowers are a staple of natural magic. Whether the witch is cutting them from the garden to decorate her altar, or putting together a healing posy for a sick friend, floral tributes are a type of magic in and of themselves. Most of us have experienced the joy of being presented with an unexpected bunch of flowers and pretty blooms are a great way to express an emotion when words might fail you. Natural witches take this one step further, by adding an intention to their flower magic, giving the blooms a specific purpose, be that attracting love when throwing rose petals into bath water, or offering strength and healing with a gift of potted lavender. Flowers can be used in many ways to enhance your nature witchery. Here are a few suggestions to get you started.

◇ Profile flowers and herbs and their magical attributes in a special book. Simply press the plants, then fix them into a blank journal and write out the meaning and magical uses of the plant next to the pressed flowers.

◇ Add dried petals and blooms to homemade incense for a magical atmosphere.

◇ Add dried plants and flowers to spell pouches and poppets.

◇ Make magical oils by placing fresh flowers, such as calendula or lavender, into a bottle and filling it with almond or sunflower oil. These bottles will make a pretty display in your witch's pantry or kitchen and you can use the oils to anoint spell candles or add to recipes for candle- and soap-making.

◇ Pressed flowers can be included in your diary, Book of Shadows or used to decorate handmade candles, soaps and baked goods.

A Victorian Posy

In the past, when personal hygiene and sanitation were poor, carrying fragrant flowers was a way to ward off unpleasant smells. Both ladies and gentlemen would frequently carry a small posy of flowers around with them. Also known as a tussie mussie, or a nosegay, these small posies could be held to the nose whenever a particularly bad smell pervaded the air, allowing the posy holder to enjoy the scent of flowers instead.

Tussie mussies were in use from the Middle Ages, becoming more popular throughout Tudor and Elizabethan times, but it was Queen Victoria who made them a popular fashion accessory of the day. During her reign, the Victorian posy holder was essential in any affluent woman's wardrobe, being made of fine porcelain or delicate silver and often presented as a gift by a doting suitor or relative.

You can make a tussie mussie of your own by gathering fragrant herbs and flowers into a small round posy, tying them with a ribbon and cutting the stems short. To add magic to the nosegay, choose flowers of a particular colour to draw in a specific energy, such as blue for healing, pink for self-love, red for romance and so on. Alternatively, you can construct an entire meaning by following the guide below.

The Language of Flowers

The Victorians were very keen to imbue their bouquets with *floriography*, or the language of flowers, in which each flower was thought to express a particular meaning. This effectively meant that there was something of an open secret being passed back and forth in Victorian society, via the bouquets that were being gifted. This practice is often referenced in popular literature and poetry of that time. It can be used to good effect in floral spells and rituals. Simply choose to use the flowers where the meaning most closely aligns with your magical desire and intention. The language of flowers is well documented and there are many books available which go into great detail regarding floriography if you want to delve deeper into this topic. For now, here is a small sample of meanings for some popular flowers and plants to get your started.

- ◇ Azalea – duty to family comes first
- ◇ Acacia – secret love
- ◇ Bluebell – constancy
- ◇ Bramble – resilience, protection, autumn
- ◇ Buttercup – childishness
- ◇ Carnation – admiration, unrequited love
- ◇ Clover – industry, luck through hard work
- ◇ Daisy – innocence
- ◇ Dandelion – oracle, faithfulness, sun and moon
- ◇ Elder-blossom – compassion, wise woman skills
- ◇ Evergreens – abundance, prosperity, winter
- ◇ Forget-me-not – true love, spring time
- ◇ Foxglove – ambition, aspiration, insincerity
- ◇ Geranium – melancholy, recollection, reflection
- ◇ Gentian – unjust
- ◇ Harebell – submission

- ◇ Heather – solitude
- ◇ Henbane – imperfection, dangerous attraction
- ◇ Iris – message of hope
- ◇ Ivy – fidelity
- ◇ Jasmine – amiable, friendly
- ◇ Lavender – healing, answers, distrust
- ◇ Lilac – first love
- ◇ Marigold – grief, sorrow
- ◇ Morning Glory – obstinacy
- ◇ Narcissus – ego, self-absorption, self-interest, self-destruction

- ◇ Nightshade – secrets, danger, vengeance
- ◇ Oak – strength, endurance, summer
- ◇ Orchid – beauty, frailty, fragility
- ◇ Pansy – thoughts, visions
- ◇ Poppy – remembrance, sleep, silence, dreams
- ◇ Ragwort – child's play, immaturity
- ◇ Rose – red – true love; yellow – infidelity, disdain; pink – self-love; white – rebellion
- ◇ Sunflower – haughtiness,
- ◇ Sweet William (Stinking Billy) – treachery, betrayal, battle
- ◇ Thistle – defiance, defence, retaliation, retribution
- ◇ Tulip – do you like me too? An invitation to an affair (especially when mixed with yellow roses!)
- ◇ Violet – modesty, steadfastness, shyness
- ◇ Water Lily – pure-hearted
- ◇ Willow – pretentiousness, downfall, reap as you've sown
- ◇ Yarrow – a declaration of war, conflict (especially when mixed with Sweet William)
- ◇ Yew – death, rebirth, ancestors

Floromancy

Floromancy is the art of divination or fortune-telling, using flowers, leaves and petals. Many people have plucked the petals from a daisy to determine if someone loves them or not, but there are lots of other ways to use flowers for fortune-telling purposes. Here are just a few.

◇ Take two potted marigold flowers and place them on a sunny window sill. Label one pot Yes and the other No. Stand before them and ask a question which requires a simple yes/no reply. Keep an eye on the flowers and as the sun sets, see which flower closes first and note which pot it is in, to find your answer.

◇ As blossom or leaves start to fall from trees, pick out a single leaf or petal and make a wish. If you finish making your wish before the petal lands on the ground it will come true; if not, it won't.

◇ Whenever you see the first flower of spring it will determine your fortune for the rest of the year. To see it on a Monday means good luck, Tuesday means success, Wednesday means a marriage within the year, Thursday means you should be careful and cautious, Friday means prosperity, Saturday means misfortune will dog at your heels and Sunday means great opportunities and lucky chances.

◇ Tradition states that the first letter of the first flower you find in spring will also be the first initial of a new love interest.

◇ Having an odd number of cut flowers in a vase is considered lucky.

◇ Floral superstitions also denote that having white lilies in the home is bad luck as they are associated with funerals.

◇ Lilac should never be cut for indoors or this will anger the fey folk.

◇ A mix of red and white flowers is also considered bad luck as in some cultures these are the colours of funeral wreaths

◇ Wearing or growing the flower of your birth month is thought to bring good luck to you.

January – Carnation
February – Violet
March – Daffodil
April – Daisy
May – Lily of the Valley
June – Rose
July – Cornflower
August – Poppy
September – Gladioli
October – Marigold
November – Chrysanthemum
December – Holly

How to Make a Midsummer Flower Crown

Items required: florists wire, wire cutters, ribbon, flowers of your choice

Timing: make on midsummer's day

It is traditional in pagan circles to make and wear a flower crown on Midsummer's Day. They are easy enough to make. All you need to do is wrap florists wire around your head two or three times to make a crown of the correct size. Twist the end of the wire around the crown to secure it, the begin to weave your chosen flowers into the wire circlet, securing with additional florist wire if necessary. You can use bright gold and orange flowers to represent the sun being at its strongest, or you can choose flower colours that match your intention, so blue for healing, pink for self-love, white for new beginnings, green for abundance and so on. Once you have placed all your flowers around the crown, add ribbon to decorate and to cover any sharp stems, tying the ends into a pretty bow at the back of the crown. Then wear the crown as part of your midsummer solstice celebrations.

Essential Oils

If you do not have access to fresh flowers, then essential oils are your new best friends! Not only do they hold all the same magical attributes as the fresh flowers, they take up less space and can be used all year round, so you don't need to wait for them to come into season. Most witches have a collection of essential oils because they are so useful.

In magic, essential oils are used to anoint spell candles, poppets and pouches. They can be simmered to fragrance a room, or added to water to create room sprays or eco-friendly cleaning products. In addition, they can be used when making your own candles, soaps, lotions and potions, plus they have the added benefit of making good massage blends for aromatherapy.

There are lots of different essential oils for you to choose from, but some of the most useful are lavender, tea-tree, ylang-ylang, eucalyptus, peppermint, bergamot, rose geranium, patchouli, clary-sage and chamomile. Keep your oils in a dark place, maybe in a wooden box or a cupboard and remember that a little goes along way. Bear in mind that most oils, with the exception of lavender and tea-tree, need to be diluted in a carrier such as almond oil before applying to the skin. Essential oils are a vital part of any witch's kit, so treat yourself to one or two and start to experiment with them in your spellcraft.

PART
7

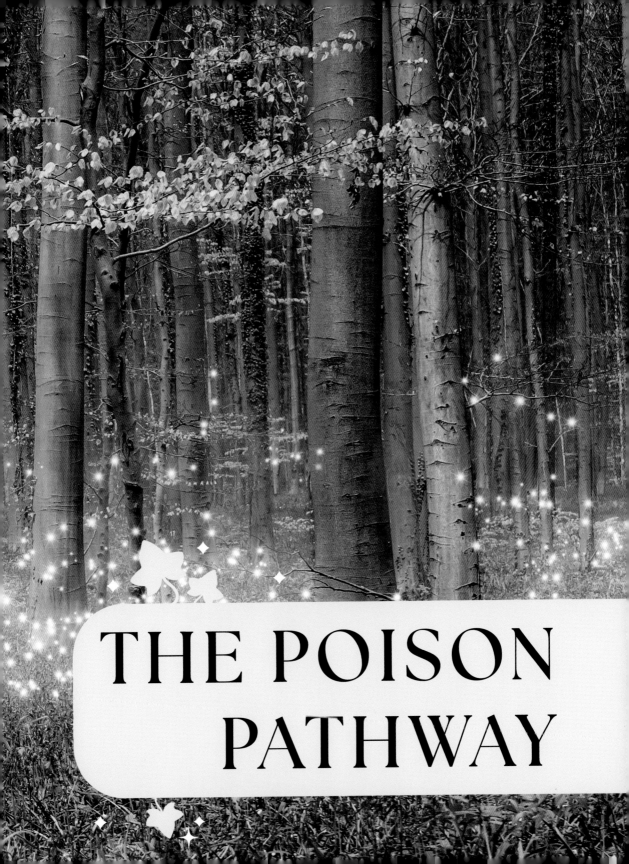

THE POISON PATHWAY

Not all plants are beneficial. Some are dangerous, even lethal, to both humans and animals. In the wrong hands such plants can be weaponized as poisons, which is what Catherine de Medici had a reputation for doing – using witch's plants to poison her rivals and political opponents. To this day, poison is still attributed as being a woman's weapon of choice for murder, though this is disputed among criminologists and could simply be a lingering form of misogyny.

Many toxic plants grow wild in woodlands and hedgerows. Some might even be growing in your own garden without you being aware of their power to harm. However, it cannot be denied that some of the most toxic and dangerous plants have long been associated with witches and witchcraft, so it is wise to know what they are so that you can avoid them and practice safely.

The Poison Garden

The Poison Garden is part of the Alnwick country estate in Northumberland, in the UK. It is a beautiful landscaped garden with a deadly difference, because all of the plants there are poisonous and harmful. Kept safely locked away, behind tall black iron gates which bear the symbol of the skull and crossbones to denote the toxicity of the garden, it has a very foreboding appearance, befitting the lethal power of the plants within. You can only see the garden by guided tour, as it would be too dangerous to allow people to wander around freely. The most interesting thing about the garden though, is that it looks so pretty and many of the poisonous plants growing there are quite common, including foxgloves and laurel. It just goes to show that common garden plants often have a darker side that we might not be aware of, so it pays to be mindful and to do your research thoroughly when dealing with plants.

Witch's Herbs

There are several plants which immediately make people think of witches and witchcraft and they are known as *witch's herbs*. Hemlock, belladonna, henbane and mandrake are all closely associated with the magical arts and all of them are lethal! Of course, no plant is the sole agent of its toxicity – it needs human intervention to administer it, and whether this be via an accidental berry-picking excursion or a pre-meditated homicide, these plants need human hands to cause harm and death.

That said, only a fool would underestimate the power of such plants, so if you plan to grow them or pick them from the wilderness, always wear surgical gloves and wash your hands thoroughly afterwards, as ingesting even a small amount can have a very harmful effect. Also be aware that while is isn't illegal to grow poisonous plants in your garden, you should not allow them to spread onto neighbours' gardens or grass verges. You will also be held responsible should any children or pets ingest them and be harmed as a result. As most of these plants grow in the wild anyway, it might be safest to just admire them from afar!

Belladonna

Atropa belladonna or *deadly nightshade* as it is more commonly known, is widespread throughout the UK, Europe and parts of America. All parts of deadly nightshade are lethal, from root to flower tip and just a small number of berries ingested is enough to kill a child. This plant prefers damp soil and thrives in woodlands, meadows and riverside spots, so those are the kind of areas where you are likely to find it growing wild. It can be identified by its purple, bell-like flowers and extremely shiny black berries.

Due to the hallucinogenic properties of belladonna, it is one of the plants that is associated with witches *flying ointment,* which was a concoction of psychoactive plants reduced to an ointment that was then administered to cause the sensation of flying. However, belladonna is so toxic that just touching it without gloves can cause painful blisters, so one wonders what the side effects to such a flying ointment might have been!

In mythology, deadly nightshade is linked to the Crone aspect of the goddess and in particular to Atropos of the Fates and Skuld of the Norns, who both sever the thread of life, so it is a plant that is inherently associated with death and its potential to cause it. Belladonna's witchy history is celebrated on the night of Walpurgis, April 30th, also known as Witches Night or May's Eve.

Henbane

Another member of the nightshade family is *Hyoscyamus niger* or *henbane,* also known as *stinking nightshade* due to its pungent, somewhat fishy smell. It grows wild in waterlogged places such as riversides, dykes and ditches and can be identified by the creamy yellow trumpet flowers that are black at the centre. Like its cousin, belladonna, all parts of henbane are poisonous and lethal if ingested. Again, it is thought to have been used as part of *flying ointment,* due to its power to induce visions and delirium, although too much can lead to madness and death, so I do not recommend trying to recreate this ointment! Historically, henbane was used to tip poison arrows by the Gauls and Greeks, while the Druids and Vikings used the plant in death rituals and funeral rites. In Greek mythology henbane was added to the potions made by the enchantress Medea.

Hemlock

Conium maculatum or *hemlock* is associated with funeral rites, particularly in Germanic regions. It thrives in watery ground along rivers and can spring up just about anywhere that is left undisturbed. It is a hardy plant, commonly known as *poison parsley* because its leaves resemble the harmless culinary herb and mistakes can prove fatal. Hemlock can be identified by its pretty white flowers in spring and summer, while its stems have purple or red spots on them. In Christian mythology these spots were said to have been the blood of Jesus as the hemlock plant grew on the site of his crucifixion. As a result, hemlock was cursed to be a fatally poisonous plant. Touching hemlock without gloves can cause bouts of dizziness and vertigo. It can cause impotence in men, as well as convulsions, hallucinations, delirium, comas and a slow death for either gender, so it is not a plant to meddle with. In ancient Greece, hemlock was the weapon of choice for state executions, its most famous victim being Socrates.

Wolfsbane

Aconitum or *wolfsbane*, also known as *monkshood* is a lovely plant with purple or yellow flowers that resemble the hood of a monk's habit. It is often found in herbaceous borders as many people are not aware of its high level of toxicity and it is attractive to bees and butterflies. All parts of wolfsbane are poisonous and it is sometimes referred to as *the queen of poisons!* In the past it was used to kill wolves, particularly in agricultural areas, hence the name wolfsbane. Again, the juice of this plant has been used to tip poison arrows and it has been by turns, said to both cure and cause lycanthropy.

Wormwood

This is the plant of the *green fairy! Artemisia absinthium* or *wormwood* is the key ingredient in the poet's draught, absinthe. *Le fee vert*, or the green fairy, is said to be the spirit of the wormwood plant and can be communed with by drinking absinthe. This fairy was thought to offer the gift of inspiration, hence the popularity of absinthe among artists, poets and writers during the Romantic period. The plant's botanical name links it with the goddess Artemis, who is associated with the hunt and therefore the woods and foliage. Wormwood was used as an antiseptic and to treat intestinal worms!

Mandrake

Mandragora officinarum or *mandrake* is an iconic plant associated with witchcraft. Both the roots and leaves are highly toxic. However, the humanoid form of the root meant that it was perfect to use as a poppet in spell casting. A member of the nightshade family, mandrake has similar hypnotic and hallucinogenic properties to belladonna and henbane. In the past it was used as a sedative and tranquilizer. Carrying a mandrake root was also said to bring good fortune, though to pull one up by the roots and hear its scream would cause instant death, so presumably you would have to get someone *else* to harvest this particular good luck charm on your behalf! Mandragora isn't a native species to the UK, so sometimes bryony roots would be used as a magical substitute. In folklore, mandrake was said to thrive in the bloody soil of execution sites, gallows and battle fields.

Fly Agaric Fairy Rings

Amanita muscaria is the red and white spotted *fly agaric* mushroom, which is synonymous with magic and fairy enchantment. It is a native fungi of the UK and they grow in woodlands from late summer to autumn. Historically they were used as pesticides to kill flies. They are highly poisonous and psychoactive, causing hallucinations, vomiting, seizures and delirium. They are probably the prettiest and most easily recognisable of all mushrooms, due in part to their appearance in children's books and fairy-tales, where they are usually depicted as being fairy homes and thrones. In folklore a ring of fly agaric mushrooms, also known as a *fairy ring*, is said to be a portal into the land of the Fey. If you find such a ring then you have been invited to dance with the fairies, but if you eat or drink anything whilst in the fairy realm, you will never be able to return to your own world. The toxic properties of fly agaric mushrooms were also used in witch's flying ointment and could account for the tales of fairy revels that are associated with this magical toadstool.

So there you have it – some the most poisonous plants associated with witchcraft. It should go without saying that this chapter is for information only and I do not recommend that you experiment with any of these plants. But it is always useful to be able to identify them, especially when you are out in woods foraging, because mistakes can be lethal. Take care and use your common sense.

PART
8

ENVIRONMENTALISM

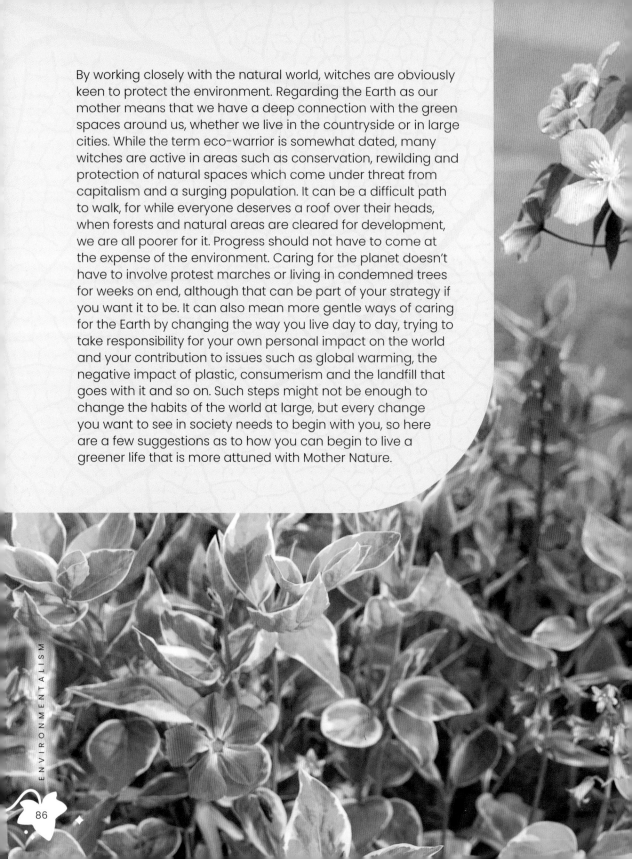

By working closely with the natural world, witches are obviously keen to protect the environment. Regarding the Earth as our mother means that we have a deep connection with the green spaces around us, whether we live in the countryside or in large cities. While the term eco-warrior is somewhat dated, many witches are active in areas such as conservation, rewilding and protection of natural spaces which come under threat from capitalism and a surging population. It can be a difficult path to walk, for while everyone deserves a roof over their heads, when forests and natural areas are cleared for development, we are all poorer for it. Progress should not have to come at the expense of the environment. Caring for the planet doesn't have to involve protest marches or living in condemned trees for weeks on end, although that can be part of your strategy if you want it to be. It can also mean more gentle ways of caring for the Earth by changing the way you live day to day, trying to take responsibility for your own personal impact on the world and your contribution to issues such as global warming, the negative impact of plastic, consumerism and the landfill that goes with it and so on. Such steps might not be enough to change the habits of the world at large, but every change you want to see in society needs to begin with you, so here are a few suggestions as to how you can begin to live a greener life that is more attuned with Mother Nature.

ENVIRONMENTALISM

How to Live a Greener Life

Living a greener life is all about making small changes to your daily routine until those changes become your new habit. Green living, or slow living, can be a welcome escape from the frenetic world we live in. By simply slowing down your life and being more mindful of the things you do and how that impacts the world around you, you will begin to feel more in tune with nature, rather than separate from it. Here are a few ideas for you try out to get started with a greener way of living.

◇ Walk as much as possible. Walk to work if you can, or walk the kids to school, instead of driving. See this walk as a time to breathe in the fresh air and to notice the world around you, the changes in the trees, the birds building nests etc. You miss all this when driving a car.

◇ If you can't walk to work, cycle there instead. Or use public transport and do some discreet people watching. Who are your fellow passengers? Try to imagine what kind of lives they lead and how their day differs from yours.

◇ Borrow, don't buy. This one is a great change to make for all those things that you would normally buy without a second thought, so if you love books, use the local libraries in your area, or see if you can swap your old books for used ones in a used book store. Swap clothes with friends and family, or start a swap group with people who have similar interests and needs. For instance, you could get a group of mothers together so that you can swap maternity clothes, or baby items.

- Recycle and repurpose old items to give them a new lease of life. Sometimes all something needs is a coat of paint and a bit of imagination. If you are artistic, try painting flowers, animals and woodland scenes on old items of furniture to make it entirely unique and something only you have, which represents your witchcore vibes.

- Donate as much as you can. We all have things that we no longer use or need, so instead of throwing them away, donate them to a charity shop, a shelter or somewhere similar. Sadly, these days there are food, baby, pet and clothing banks springing up all over the place, so donating your unwanted items there will ensure that they go to people who need them most.

- Go foraging for mushrooms, nuts and berries, instead of buying them at the supermarket.

- Grow your own produce if you have the space. You don't need a huge space to grow a small crop of tomatoes or strawberries. Grow your own herbs for spellcraft and cooking.

- Let the grass grow, allow part of your garden to grow wild, or plant a wildflower garden. This will encourage bees and other pollinating insects to your garden. Pretty flowers will attract pretty butterflies so it's a win-win situation.

- Try to eat less meat and dairy, or adopt a vegan diet if you can stomach it.

- Avoid using plastic, so take your own bags to the supermarket, use a reusable drinking bottle or cup and invest in reusable straws.

- Have a Witch-Swap with like-minded friends and swap crystals, card decks and magical tools. Just remember to ritually cleanse your new treasures before you use them.

Casting Spells for the Environment

As well as trying to reduce their own negative impact on the environment, witches also like to cast spells to protect it. This type of magic takes many forms, from invoking guardian spirits to watch over threatened trees and green spaces, to casting for the ethical and humane treatment of livestock.

It makes sense that a witch would use magic to address these issues, because she is in effect using her own spiritual power to heal and protect the greater power of the Earth, which she connects with in her magic. This kind of symbiosis carries with it the responsibility to act as a guardian of the earth when necessary. This could be something as simple as a dispute with a neighbour who wants you to cut down the trees growing in your garden because *he* doesn't like them, in which case you would need to defend their right to grow and to be there in the first place. Or it could be more complex, in the form of a co-ordinated spell with other witches to protect an area from development. Witchcraft is the art of transformation by spell work, so making magic to transform the damage done to the Earth is the responsibility of every witch.

Blessing of Sacrifice

Whether you are vegetarian, vegan or not, farming animals for the food industry is a fact of life all over the world. These animals should be honoured for their sacrifice, even if you do not eat meat yourself, and they should be defended and protected against any cruel or inhumane treatment, including during their slaughter.

The full moon of October is known as the Blood Moon, because this was traditionally the time when livestock would be slaughtered and salted in order to provide meat for the coming winter months. This was a kind of ritual slaughter, where the animals were honoured for their sacrifice. In modern farming, animals are routinely sent to the slaughter house and meat is readily available throughout the year for those that choose to eat it. Any moon could be a blood moon for modern farm animals and it is a great shame that their sacrifice goes largely unnoticed and is taken for granted. One thing green witches can do is honour the spirits of slaughtered livestock, as not only does this mark their sacrifice, it also connects us to our pagan ancestors. The spell on page 92 is designed to bless and honour the livestock that is destined for the food industry.

Blessing for Livestock

Items required:
- ◇ one black candle
- ◇ one red candle
- ◇ red thread
- ◇ a plate to hold them

Moon Phase:
- ◇ cast on the Blood/Full Moon of October or on Samhain

You will need two candles, one black and one red. Tie them both together with a piece of red thread and stand them on a plate, using a little melted wax from the bottom of the candles to secure them in place. Hold your hands over the candles and say:

I honour the passing of all slaughtered beasts

Who give their lives so that we might feast

With honour and reverence, respect and love

I give thanks to the creatures of Earth and the powers above.

Blessed be and thank you for your sacrifice.

Light both the candles and leave them in place until they have burnt out naturally. Give extra thanks for any meat-based dishes that make up your diet.

Share the Love Spell

Items required:
- ◇ an apple
- ◇ athame or knife
- ◇ pentacle
- ◇ water

Moon Phase:
- ◇ perform during a waxing moon

This is a great little spell to give your love to Earth Mother, by sharing an apple, the fruit of love, with the Earth. Take an apple out to a natural spot, such as your garden or a woodland. Cut the apple in half across the equator line, to expose the five-pointed star of seeds at the centre. Scoop out the seeds and place them on the pentacle as you eat one half of the apple. Then say:

This fruit of love I give to the earth

That she may give these seeds rebirth

Apples green and apples red

Come into bloom from your earthly bed

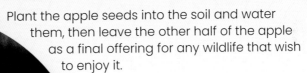

Plant the apple seeds into the soil and water them, then leave the other half of the apple as a final offering for any wildlife that wish to enjoy it.

Spell to Protect a Tree

Items required:
◇ lavender oil
◇ a small cat's bell
◇ red thread

Moon Phase:
◇ full moon

If you know of any tree that is under threat of being cut down, cast this spell to help protect it. On the night of the full moon, go out to the tree, taking with you a small cat's bell hung on a length of red thread and a bottle of lavender essential oil. Place your hands on the trunk of the tree and send your loving strength into the bark. Visualize a green light passing from your palms into the tree trunk and lighting up the tree from the inside. Next hang the bell from one of the branches with the red thread and as you do so say:

Ring out danger, ring out harm

Ring out loud and sound the alarm

When woodsmen come to chop and fell

Their work is thwarted by this spell

Long life to this tree, protected be

Long life to this tree, so shall it be!

As a final step, draw the Algiz protection rune (ᛉ) onto the tree trunk using the lavender oil, then bless the tree and know that you have done what you can to cast a spell of protection around it. Whatever the outcome, the spirit of the tree will know that you tried to help.

Invoke a Land Deva

Items required:
◇ a stone or crystal

Moon Phase:
◇ full moon

If you know that an area is under threat from developers or vandals, then invoking a land deva is a good way to keep such intruders away. Land devas are spirits of the earth and guardians of the green. Their presence can be enough to scare away those who come to the area with bad intentions.
To invoke a land deva to protect a tree or a green space, go to the area and sit on the ground. Close your eyes and visualize the deva of the land rising up from the earth in front of you and say:

Spirit of Earth, I invoke you to protect this sacred space

Let none come here with ill intent, but make them flee before you

Help us to keep this area green and growing, its life energies free and flowing

Wild and untamed, free and unfettered, send intruders away until they learn better

May your presence and the magic imbued in this stone keep this place green and whole

So mote it be.

Leave the stone or crystal in a hidden place within the area that you are trying to protect.

PART
9

ACTIVISM &
EMPOWERMENT

Natural magic practitioners are often involved in activism, as well as environmentalism. While they do cast spells for the protection of the natural world, as activists, witches also cast for the improvement of society, both at home and abroad. This could mean working spells for the demise of terrorist organisations, or rituals to uphold the rights of women. In this respect, witchcraft meets politics and many a witch has penned her signature on petitions for issues that concern society at large.

While on the surface it might seem as if political issues have little or nothing to do with witchcraft, in fact nothing could be further from the truth. We all have to live in the society which we create, both locally and globally. The internet has also had a big impact, because it has made us more aware of what is going on in other parts of the world, and the tensions and conflicts that people are having to endure. Witchery is a good way to send out positive energy to the places that need it most and it can be as simple as lighting a candle and sending love to the world.

Modern Witch Hunts

Although witches are free to practice their craft safely here in the west, in some parts of the world, witch hunts are still going on. We might like to believe that witch hunting has been consigned to the history books, but in places like Africa, Brazil and India, people are still being accused of witchcraft. Just as with the witch-craze of the past, the majority of those accused in modern witch hunts tend to be elderly women or sometimes children – people who are vulnerable and therefore easy targets. In some countries, witch trials are actually taking place in courts, or in village tribunals, that have been set up for that specific purpose. It seems unbelievable that such trials have any place in the modern world, but sadly, they do. Lynching is not uncommon, along with beatings and torture that becomes increasingly brutal. Accused witches are frequently forced to drink toxic potions that are thought to rid them of evil spirits, but which are often so poisonous the accused dies. In some parts of the world just owning an amulet or good luck charm is enough to get you killed for a witch! Western witches can help by raising awareness of this issue, using social media platforms and of course we can also cast spells.

Spell to Let the Hunters Become the Hunted

Items required:
◇ an image of Artemis
◇ a tea light candle and holder

Moon Phase:
◇ full moon

Artemis is the goddess of the hunt and mythology states that when she caught huntsman Actaeon watching her bathe in a lake, she turned him into a stag and he was killed by his own hounds. In this spell we call on Artemis to help us to turn the tide against the modern day witch hunters. Take the image of Artemis and in front place the tea light in the holder. Light the candle and concentrate on the image of the goddess. Imagine her retribution being paid out to the witch hunters as you say the incantation below three times.

Let the hunters be hunted, let the victims run free

Let the witches be valiant while their persecutors flee

Let the arrows of Artemis strike at their hearts

As the foe of all witches, the witch-hunter departs!

So mote it be.

Protests

In recent years we have seen a surge of public empowerment with marches and protests at the systemic sexism, misogyny and racism that pervades society. These movements have led in part to a society which is becoming more aware of these underlying issues. People are having to reassess how they behave. They are having to adjust how they interact with others and be more inclusive.

Large organizations are finally beginning to understand that they cannot simply brush sexual harassment or racism under the rug as they might have done before. The public will no longer stand for it and these organizations will be held accountable for the actions of the people who work beneath such banners and logos.

Abuse of any kind should never be tolerated in society and when someone in a position of power uses that power to abuse others, then that is a serious transgression which must be tackled and brought to light, regardless of if that person is a politician or a pilot, a police officer, a soldier or a celebrity. Fame, fortune and diplomatic immunity should offer them no protection when they abuse their position.

Furthermore, it can be incredibly damaging for a victim to have to watch their abuser win promotions, accolades and celebrity status, when their own life lies in tatters around them, because someone abused their position. Sadly, we have seen what the consequences are when such behaviour goes unchallenged. The spell on page 102 is designed to keep the bad apples in check. Use it in conjunction with the *Spell to Let the Hunter Become the Hunted* opposite for the best results.

Spell for Binding Those Who Abuse Their Power

Items required:
- ◇ an apple
- ◇ athame or knife
- ◇ garlic powder

Moon Phase:
- ◇ waning moon

Take the apple and, using the athame, carve into the apple skin the name of the abuser, along with the organization they are connected to. Sprinkle the apple with garlic powder to banish their behaviour, then bury the apple deep in the earth as you say:

Misunderstandings are no excuse

I shine a light on your abuse

Misdemeanours you've hidden well

But I have a voice, I'll show and tell!

I'll blow the whistle to end your game

Let the truth be known, you're named and shamed.

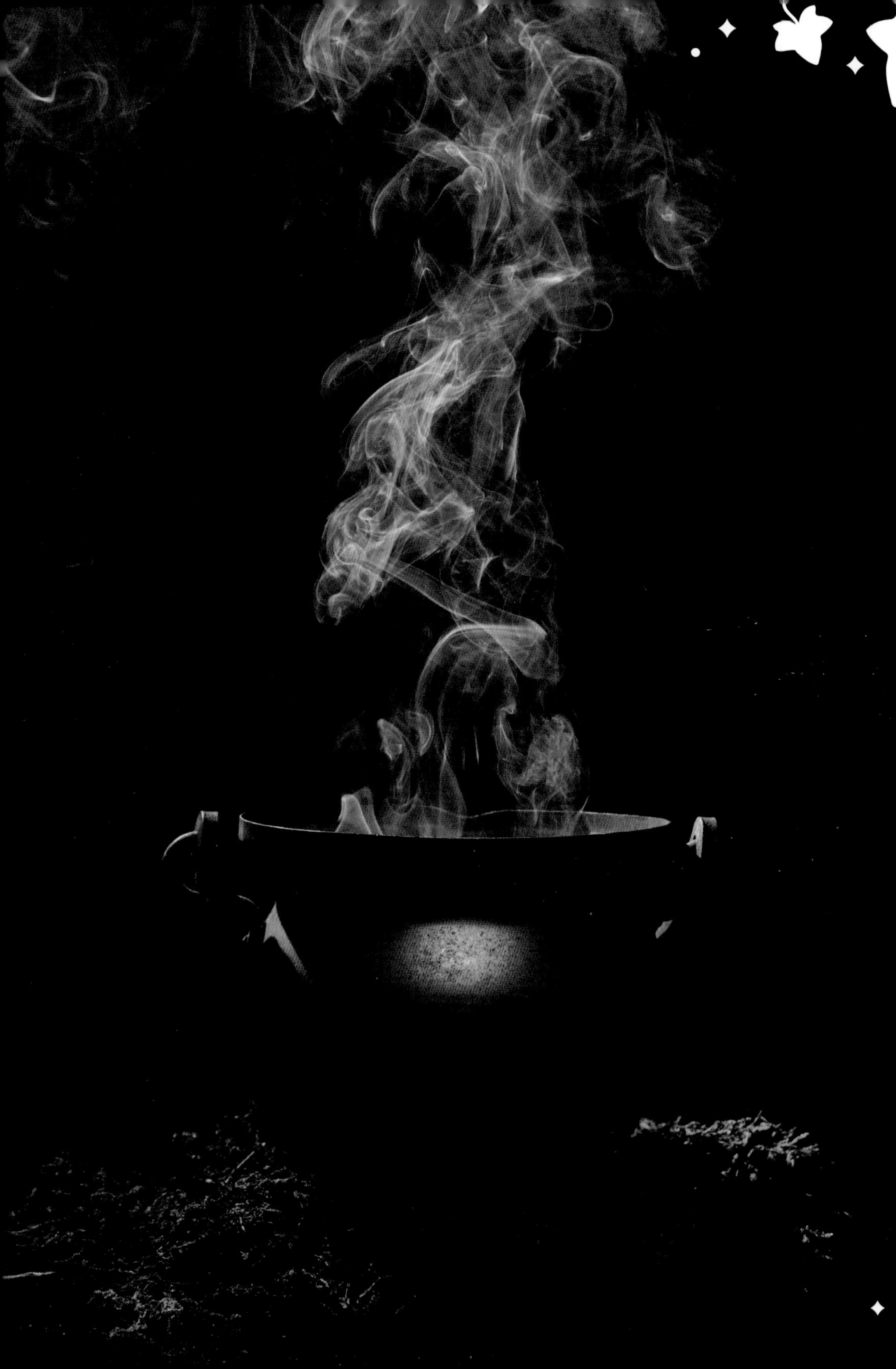

Diversity and Tolerance

There is no doubt that society is changing and at a rapid pace. It can be hard to keep up and even harder to stay on the right side of what is currently viewed as being politically correct. Social interactions can be a minefield and an innocent remark can quickly blow up in your face to become so much more. This is especially true for those of us who are quite outspoken! Suddenly it seems as if everyone is looking for an opportunity to be offended, and while people do have the *right* to be offended by something you say, they *do not* have the right to *choose* your words for you! Of course, I am not suggesting that you go out of your way to be mean, spiteful or deliberately offensive to people. What I *am* saying is that society is made up of so many different cultures and points of view that it is inevitable that people will clash at some point.

Diversity is one of the great strengths of modern society. Think how boring the world would be if we were all exactly the same. That said, it can at times be quite difficult to truly empathise with someone who is on a completely different path than you are. But here's the thing – you don't have to *understand* everyone's perspective in depth. You don't have to understand all the complex mental and emotional needs that set someone on the transgender or non-binary path, for instance. You just have to step back and let them get on with it, so that they feel free and safe to live the life of *their* choice. That's it. That's all you have to do, is live and let live, with harm to none.

Live And Let Live Spell

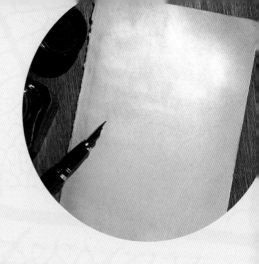

Item required:
◇ a piece of paper and a pen
◇ a cauldron or heat proof dish
◇ lighter

Moon Phase:
◇ full moon

This simple spell calls for a more tolerant society, as well as being a reminder to yourself to be more tolerant and understanding towards people who are living a different kind of life. You do not know what struggles anyone else is enduring, so be kind to others and cast this spell for wider tolerance in your community. Write the following incantation on a piece of paper, chant it three times, then burn the paper in the cauldron to release the spell.

All colours, all creeds, all loves be as one

All nations, all notions of self, redone

All styles, all images, viewed as an art

All spirits and religions that come from the heart

Live and let live in love and in trust

Live and let live, tolerance is a must.

Refuse to be Silenced!

While we should be kind to those who are on a different path to us, it is also important not to allow yourself to be silenced simply for fear of causing offence. You have every right to form and present your own opinions, providing you do so respectfully. However, these days it can feel like we are in danger of being shouted down whenever we voice an unpopular opinion and this is dangerous, because silencing people is usually the first step in any dictatorship. Freedom to speak your mind, to have a free Press who hold governments accountable for their actions, is a vital part of any democratic society. Without free speech we are a mute nation of bystanders. With free speech, we are a nation of activists and protestors and a force to be reckoned with!

Speak Your Truth Spell

Items required:
- ◇ a white candle and holder
- ◇ a lighter

Moon Phase:
- ◇ new moon

Cast this spell whenever you feel the need to get something off your chest, or to speak up for others in society. It's a good one to cast the night before attending any protest march too. Light the white candle and focus on the flame as you imagine getting your point across, peacefully, but with conviction. Visualize the changes that might come to pass if your opinions are taken seriously and your suggestions acted upon. When you can see this clearly in your mind, repeat the following chant three times, then let the candle burn down naturally.

Blessed be those who are different

Blessed be those who are the same

Blessed be my voice raised in protest

Blessed be those who are blamed

In love and in trust I break silence

In valour and strength, I face fear

In peaceful, harmonious cadence

I speak out my truth with a cheer!

PART
10

GREEN LIVING AND GIVING

Giving back to the earth is all part of natural magic, so along with spells for environmental and activism issues, witches often work locally to give a bit of their energy back to the green spaces around them. In this chapter, we are going to look at simple ways you can give back to Mother Nature who nurtures all of us so well.

Adopt a Tree

Taking special interest in a tree in your local area is one way to reconnect with the nature of your environment. See this as a kind of voluntary adoption and begin to spend time near the tree, learning about it and bringing offerings to place at its roots. Young saplings are great for children to adopt because they grow so quickly, like children do. Older trees can make wise companions and are great for meditating beneath, or just sitting close and contemplating. Feed the roots with libations of cider or ale, perhaps sharing a tipple each evening as you walk the dog. Trace runes of protection on the bark and hang food for the birds from its branches. Eventually you will feel that you have made a true friend in the tree and your symbiotic relationship will begin to thrive.

Litter Bug Buster

Taking part in a litter picking session, or organizing one with your friends, is another way that natural witches give back. You can even do this as a solitary practice, taking a bin bag and picking up the litter in an untidy part of your local community. Spending an hour pulling empty crisps packets and sweet wrappers from the hedgerows as you walk back from dropping the kids off at school, is a good way to show an environmental awareness and to teach your children to be more aware, too. For larger, organised litter picking, you may need permission from your local council, who can also provide you with some useful equipment to help the job along. Make sure to keep a first aid kit with you in case of accidents from broken glass or tin cans.

Create a Community Garden

If there is a small area of waste land near your home, seek permission from the council to turn it into a community garden and start to plant flowers and herbs. Tend the garden well, so that the council can see this is an asset to the area and gather friends and neighbours to help you weed and plant. In this way you are creating a pretty green space that everyone can enjoy. As an alternative, you could use an allotment to grow vegetables and then donate them to food banks or soup kitchens.

A Forest Witch Tea-Party

Items required:

◇ a picnic basket and blanket

◇ your favourite sandwiches, cakes and juice to drink, nuts, seeds, apples, peanut butter

◇ a few large pine cones

◇ florists' wire or thread

◇ athame or knife

Moon Phase:

◇ a summery day during a waxing moon is best

Is there anything more enchanting than enjoying a tea-party picnic in the woods? It feels like the kind of thing the witches of old would have done, and whether you go alone or with friends, there is something very spiritual about taking food out into the forest and inviting your woodland friends to partake with you. For this ritual, you are going to pack a basket with all good things to eat, but your picnic will be one with a difference, for you are going to be making food for the birds, squirrels and deer to enjoy, as well as for yourself.

To begin, wrap florists' wire around each of the pine cones, leaving enough wire at the top to hang it from. Then fill the pine cones with peanut butter, spreading it quite thickly all around the cone. Next roll the buttered pine cone through a mixture of seeds suitable for wild birds. Put the cones into a lunchbox and keep them in the fridge overnight.

On the day of the forest tea-party, make your favourite sandwiches and fill your picnic basket with sweet cakes and something to drink. Next add a bag of mixed nuts suitable for wildlife, the buttered pine cones from the fridge, apples, a jar of runny honey, a saucer and the athame. Throw a picnic blanket and a good book on top and you are ready to go out into the woods. Once there, spread out your blanket and invite your woodland friends to tea with the following incantation.

Friends of fur, friends of air,

I offer up these gifts to share

A picnic here I place this day

Feel free to come and sit and stay

Nuts and fruits and seeds and treats

Come join with me, as good things we eat!

All are welcome!

Blessed be.

Hang the pine cones from the nearby trees, place piles of nuts and apple slices on the forest floor at a slight distance so that the wildlife will feel safe to enjoy them. Finally, for your insect friends, pour some honey onto the saucer and place this on the forest floor too, safely away from your own picnic area. Then sit down in the forest, eat your picnic, read your book and enjoy spending time with the wildlife. You can leave the nuts and fruit in the forest when you leave, but be sure to take the saucer and all your litter away with you. *Happy eating!*

PART
11

MOON
MANIFESTATION

All natural magic is a kind of manifestation because you are attempting to bring into being something that wasn't in your reality prior to casting the spell. You can also use it to banish something which no longer serves you and in this sense you are manifesting a void, that you can fill with something better. Witches have always manifested in tune with the moon and we cast our spells in accordance with certain phases to bring about specific results.

The moon teaches us to have patience, even when casting for our deepest desires. It is a visual reminder that magic can take time. A general rule of thumb is that smaller spells take approximately one full lunar cycle to manifest, while bigger spells may take several months. So if you were to cast for a windfall on the new moon, you might find yourself with a pay rise by the time the next new moon comes around. Likewise, if you were casting to move house or start a family on the full moon, it could be six full moons or more before this goal manifests in your life. The bigger the goal, the longer it takes, but the moon is a constant companion as you wait for the manifestation to occur, offering you a visual cue to stay positive and keep affirming your success. For the remainder of this book, we explore the power of the moon in natural magic.

Like Attracts Like

In magic, like attracts like, so what you focus on the most is what you are pulling into your life. This happens whether you are aware of it or not and it is the reason why it pays to be positive. Negative habits and thought patterns, feelings of low self-worth, disparaging self-talk and so on, can all work to bring more negative circumstances your way. Fortunately, the opposite is also true, so surrounding yourself with positive people, habits and thought processes will bring more positive circumstances towards you. Be mindful of the energies that you are sending out into the world because that is exactly the kind of energy that will come back to you. Be optimistic, positive, gentle and kind, and that is what you will attract.

Declare Your Intentions to the Moon

Making a declaration is a powerful thing. There is a reason that people remember the first time their partner said *I love you* – it's because this is a powerful declaration of an emotional bond. There is also a reason why you often say it back – because like attracts like! With this in mind, declaring your intentions to the moon can have a deep impact on your chances of success, because you are putting your goal out into the universe, confiding in the moon like an old friend.

Think of something that you want to achieve in the next month. It could be that you want to sign up to a new class, or start a new hobby, make a new friend etc. Once you have your intention in mind, go outside on the night of the full moon. Look up at the bright orb in the sky and breathe in her energies, then state your intention out loud or in your head. For example, you might say something like this: *Mother moon I greet you and welcome your light, I set my intention to take up dance classes this night.*

Now as you watch the moon move through her cycle, she will remind you each night to follow through on your intention, so that by the time she is full once more, you are already attending dance classes and living the reality of that ambition. You can repeat this process for any goal. Just remember that bigger goals will take longer than a month to manifest.

Moon Mapping

Another technique for manifesting with the moon is that of moon mapping. This is great for larger goals and is a good way to maintain focus and motivation. Think of a large goal that you would like to achieve, then break it down into smaller, achievable tasks. Write out the phases of the moon on a sheet of paper and alongside each phase, plot out the tasks of your goal, in alignment with that moon phase. So if you wanted to start a new business for example, your moon map might look something like this.

◇ New Moon: write a business plan
◇ Waxing Moon: set up a website or scout for premises
◇ Full Moon: apply for a business loan, open a business bank account and register as self-employed for tax purposes
◇ Waning Moon: hand in your notice or reduce your hours at your current job, clear out anything that isn't in alignment with your new business plan
◇ Dark Moon: conduct market research and product development for your business
◇ New Moon: start trading

This type of time structuring means that you are drawing upon the energies of the moon that are in alignment with the tasks you need to perform. You can use a moon map for any goal and you can expand the time scale so that you are mapping out several months of lunar cycles, rather than just the one as given in the example above. The beauty of this is that the lunar cycle keeps you on track with your plans, be they long or short term.

Express Gratitude

Gratitude is a vital component of all magic and manifestation, especially natural magic. Lack of gratitude can derail your spells in a heartbeat. Demonstrating that you appreciate what you already have will ensure that more comes to you. Traditionally the full moon is a propitious time to offer your gratitude to the universe, but ideally you should show that you are grateful on a daily basis. Gratitude is an active pursuit, not a passive one. Here are some ideas for demonstrating gratitude.

◇ Keep a gratitude journal and write down 3–5 things that you are grateful for each night before you go to sleep. What did the day bring that you particularly enjoyed?

◇ Light a stick of incense and allow it to burn on your altar as an offering of gratitude to the universe for all that you have.

◇ Donate to those in need, as this is a way of acknowledging that you are fortunate enough to have an excess. Clothes, books, baby things – whatever you have an abundance of, go through and donate some things to charity.

◇ Tithe to a charity by making a financial contribution each month to an organization you care about.

◇ Offer your time and do some volunteering. You could visit a nursing home and spend time with the elderly, or offer to babysit for a friend so she can have some downtime.

◇ Send a thank you note to someone who has helped you in some way.

◇ Cook a meal for someone.

◇ Feed the wildlife by putting out bird feeders and nuts for squirrels etc.

◇ Pick up litter to show gratitude for the beautiful planet we are lucky enough to call home.

◇ Show gratitude for freedom and security by assisting military veterans. Offer your time to service charities or buddy up with an ex-serviceman or woman in your area.

◇ Appreciate what you have and the people who surround you.

◇ Know that gratitude is the fastest way to experience the manifestation of your goals.

A Lunar Spell to Manifest a Dream

If there is something that you have wanted for a long time, then casting a little bit of magic can help to pull it toward you. Is there something that you have almost given up on, believing that you are not meant to have it? Or it could be that your wish was almost granted, only to be snatched away again soon afterwards. Take heart, because this is a sign that your dream is coming to you and you just need to have a little more patience. You can use this magic to draw it closer. On a new moon, begin by writing your wish on a piece of paper and then keep the paper close to your heart for seven nights. Then as the moon waxes towards full, burn the spell paper in a cauldron as you say:

My heartfelt wish is in this fire

I call on magic to lift me higher

And manifest my true desire.

Let the ashes cool down and then scatter them to the four winds to release the spell out into the universe.

How to Make Wish Incense

Burning incense is an ancient way of honouring and petitioning the gods and you can use this technique in your rituals to honour the moon. Burning incense on a daily basis is one of the simplest types of spells to cast, providing you do so with intention. It's quick, it's easy and it takes very little time to complete the ritual. It is also something that you can easily add into your evening routine when you come home from work, so that you get a touch of magic into your day.

Making your own incense means that your rituals become more potent, because you can charge the incense with a specific intention as you make it, in this case that of a Wish to help make your dreams come true.

You will need a clean empty jar and lid, a mortar and pestle, and the following dried herbs – mint, basil, lavender, calendula, tea leaf and cinnamon. These herbs are great for manifestation spells because they are said to bring good fortune and opportunity.

On the night of the new moon, place a teaspoon of each herb into the mortar and grind them together with the pestle using a clockwise motion. As you do so imagine that this incense will carry your wishes directly to the moon and her deities, who will hear your desires and help them to manifest in your life. Once the incense resembles a fine powder, pour it into the jar and label it Wish Incense. Leave the jar on a windowsill where it can soak up the moon's energies for a full lunar cycle, by which time it will be ready to use in your spellcraft.

There are several ways that you can use this incense in your magic. You can burn a pinch or two on a charcoal block as this is more traditional, or you could use it as a scattering powder and sprinkle it on your doorstep, windowsills and around your home to draw your intentions towards you. In addition, you can anoint a candle with Lunar oil (oil that is blessed by the light of a full moon) and then roll it in the incense to give a powerful boost to your candle rituals.

The Dark Side of the Moon

The dark side of the moon is the side of the moon that faces away from the Earth. It is associated with the unknown, the mysterious, spiritual rest, dark psychology, shadow work and reassessing your life. In terms of manifestation, the dark side of the moon invites you to explore your mental landscape, identify any blocks that are standing in your way and fine tune your inner circle. This lunar influence is suggestive of deep personal reflection and raises the question: *Where are you heading and who are you taking along for the ride?*

What Holds You Back?

Sometimes you can be your own worst enemy, self-sabotaging your dreams and goals with unhelpful habits such as tardiness, arrogance or apathy. This would mean that your goals always elude you, especially if you are not proactively working towards them. Nothing will ever just fall into your lap and an apathetic approach won't get you anywhere. You need to take steps to move your manifestations forward.

Fear is often something that holds people back. The idea of success can be quite a scary prospect, even if you dream of being successful! The reality of your dream might feel uncomfortable. If you have ambitions to start your own business, for instance, but the thought of being responsible for your own taxes or hiring an accountant intimidates you, then the chances are that you will subconsciously sabotage your goal, so as to avoid that level of responsibility. Just like the dark side of the moon is hidden from view, your subconscious fears are often hidden at the back of your mind, but they still have the power to derail your dreams unless you confront them. The following exercise will help you to excavate any fears you might be holding on to in relation to your goal.

Brainstorm Your Fears

Take a large sheet of paper and in the centre write a keyword that sums up your main goal. Next add any words that come into your mind, both negative and positive. Try to keep the negative words on the left side of the page and the positive ones on the right, but use up as much space as possible. Once you have all your thoughts on paper, see if you can identify any patterns. If there are more negative words then positive ones, for example, this indicates that your mind-set isn't yet in alignment with your goal, so you would need to work on thinking more positively, in terms of possibility, in order for your dream to manifest. Analyze any negative words to see if they represent variations of the same fear and think about how you can alleviate those fears, or handle the situation in a positive way should the worst happen and your fears come to pass. In this way you can see at a glance whether or not your fears are realistic, and whether your mind-set is supporting your goal or holding you back from achieving it. Once you have this knowledge, then you can begin to take steps to ensure that your mind is your strongest asset in manifestation, rather than your greatest downfall.

Your Dreams Will Wax and Wane

It is rare for people to hold only one dream for their entire life. People change and their dreams and goals change with them. What felt like a realistic goal for you at 20 might not be realistic at 60 or 70 years of age. By the same token, an aspiration you once dismissed as nothing more than a pipe-dream might actually manifest later on in life. Accomplishing one goal often leads you on to creating newer, bigger goals – and not all of them will manifest. That's okay because there will be other, more achievable, goals that will take their place. Your dreams will also change with your circumstances and the roles you take on will alter accordingly. As an example, the job that you were once very happy in may suddenly no longer suit you. It might feel too small, or too stifling because you have out-grown it, or perhaps because you were too big for it in the first place. This is a good thing, as it is a sign of your personal development. When a particular career path, job or relationship is waning for you, try not to fight it. Embrace this change and know that something better will come along to fill the void and your life will begin to wax and grow once more. Reassessing your goals regularly to see if they are still appropriate and achievable will prevent you from wasting valuable time on something that is clearly not working.

Letting Go of a Dream

Letting go of a dream that you have held on to for some time is heart-breaking, but nothing new can come into your life while you are focused on a goal that simply isn't working. In letting go, one of two things will usually happen – either the original goal will suddenly manifest out of nowhere because you stopped holding onto it so tightly or something better suited to you will come along instead.

It takes courage to let go of an ambition that isn't bearing any fruit. It can feel a lot like failure, yet all you are doing is making space in your life for whatever is *meant* to come to you instead. Be brave and let it go, trusting that the universe has other plans for you. The ritual on page 130 can help you to come to terms with a defunct ambition, helping you to release it.

A Ritual to Let Go of a Defunct Dream

You will need a few blessing seeds, also called Nigella seeds. On a waning moon, take the blessing seeds outside. Gaze at the waning moon and think about the dream that you are letting go. Consider all the things you did to try and make it manifest. Remember all the disappointments, the tears, the frustration, the rejection, the set-backs, the feeling of banging your head against a wall, of getting nowhere. Try to accept that this goal might not be part of your destiny. When you feel ready, pour a few blessing seeds into your hand and say:

I bless the dream I held so dear

I cast it from my heart

I let it go, my path to clear

Disappointment now departs

This goal no longer fills my mind

For it had no fruit to bear

I trust the moon to send in kind

A different joy to share.

Blow the blessing seeds from your hand out into the night, then turn around and walk away without looking back. Congratulations! You have now cleared the path for something wonderful to come to you instead, so allow yourself to look forward to an unknown blessing.

Fine Tune Your Inner Circle

The influences that you surround yourself with can either lift you up or drag you down and if it's the latter, then they are also blocking your ability to manifest goals. Remember that like attracts like, so if you are surrounded by negative people they will only bring that negative energy into your life and to your ambitions. This creates a block to your dreams. It's all very well being a member of a popular clique of friends, but if your inner circle is quite a toxic friend group, this can have a very damaging effect on your ability to progress in life and manifest the things you want. Reassessing your relationships is a vital step in manifestation, because you need to be free to follow your own path, rather than modifying your behaviour to suit someone else. Sadly, sometimes it is those who are closest to you who are holding you back or trying to sabotage you in some way.

Toxic people tend to be quite controlling. They want to be at the centre of your life and they try to separate you from more positive influences, which means that they become the sole source of support – or lack thereof. They will try to undermine you in whatever way they can, so if your dream is to go to university, they will try to talk you out of it, or they will disrupt your ability to study by having the TV on loudly in the next room and so on. They might even 'accidentally' destroy or damage your work. This is a subtle form of sabotage and a toxic behaviour. If friends or family members are doing their best to keep you down, sneering at your ambitions or planting the seeds of self-doubt with their concerns, then you need to limit the time you spend with such people and consider keeping your ambitions to yourself.

The Benefit of Cutting Off Toxic People

Ending a relationship that has turned toxic is never easy, but no-one is *entitled* to your friendship, especially if they have behaved in a toxic or spiteful manner towards you. Sometimes the gentlest way to extract yourself from such a situation is to allow the friendship to simply fizzle out on its own, by being too busy for gatherings or nights out together. While it can be tough to accept that your friend or family member is having a negative impact on your life and ambitions, you are always entitled to choose who you spend time with – and who you don't!

There are also certain benefits to refining your inner circle in this way, because what frequently happens when you cut away the dead wood of your life is that new shoots start to come through. Ending a toxic relationship often acts as a catalyst, projecting you forwards onto the next level of your life, where exciting new opportunities come along to fill the void. No longer weighed down with someone else's envy, spite, negative attitude or controlling demeanour, you are free to soar to greater heights. Chances are that you will become even *more* successful once you have distanced yourself from people who perhaps didn't actually have your best interests at heart after all. Just don't expect them to like you for it!

Authentic Ambition Vs A Pale Imitation

The moon has no light of her own. She has to reflect the light of the sun in order to shine. The same can be true for some people too and there will always be certain individuals who prefer to try and steal someone else's light, rather than taking the time to discover and pursue their own authentic path to success, so you will need to assess whether your goal is a genuine, authentic ambition that comes from within, or an attempt at emulating or usurping the success of someone else.

How do you know the difference? A good indication lies in the timing of your ambition. If your ambition first developed *after* someone you know has already achieved that goal, then the chances are you are imitating that person in order to try and get ahead, level up with them, or even tear them down a few pegs by proving that you can do it too! Likewise, if you prefer to stand back and watch to see if someone else can succeed at something, before you even think about giving it a try yourself, then again, you are acting from a place of imitation, rather than authenticity. This is a classic case of *you go first – I'll hold the rope!* Don't be the one who is holding the rope.

Authentic ambition does not require someone else to lay the groundwork first. An authentic ambition means that you are happy to be the first to blaze that trail yourself and to take all the risks that entails. It means that you are quite prepared to put in the time and effort it takes to succeed, rather than waiting until someone else has laid the groundwork, and then attempting to follow in their footsteps in an attempt to reap the same results.

This type of toxic imitation is not uncommon and there will always be people who try to hang off the coat tails of more successful individuals. We see it all the time in celebrity culture, even in schools where pupils try to copy homework from their friends, who they perceive as being more intelligent than themselves. However, there are several reasons why copying and imitation simply doesn't work in the long run and it is certainly not a path to manifesting lasting success. Here's why.

1   You Will Always Be Playing Catch-Up

Whenever you try to emulate someone else, you are immediately setting yourself behind the trend and you will always be struggling to catch up with the success of the people you are emulating. This means that your ideas, goals and designs will be viewed as outdated and lagging behind, which makes success more difficult to achieve.

The flip side, of course, is that the person you are emulating will always have the head start! They already *know* what they are currently working on or what they plan to do next, but *you* have to wait until they've actually done it, before you can put a similar plan into action yourself. This generally means that you will always be working six to twelve months behind the original, possibly even longer. Like it or not, this only adds to the authentic value of the original person's ideas, projects and designs! For example, it takes the high street clothing chains approximately twelve months to dupe the fashion designs they see on the catwalk, but the very fact that they emulate the big fashion houses at all, only increases the perceived value of the original authentic designs, which become more desirable for their authenticity and trend-setting power.

2   They Are Already Established in Their Field

This goes hand in hand with playing catch-up, because the person you emulate is likely to be a well-established member of their chosen field – otherwise why would you want to emulate them?! They may have been working in this field for considerable time, which means that they have spent years building a good reputation and putting together a network of professional contacts they like to work with, and who they have successfully collaborated with in the past. By the same token, the professionals in this network are more likely to want to work with their original colleague, rather than taking a chance on an unknown quantity such as yourself, which could be considered too great a risk.

3　There Is No Gap in The Market for You

Being successful in any area involves filling a gap in the market, but when you are emulating someone else's success, then that gap has already been filled by the person or company you are emulating. This effectively means that there isn't really a space for you to fill, especially if you are trying to do exactly the same kind of thing. Why would a movie producer hire a Tom Cruise or Brad Pitt lookalike fresh out of drama school, when they can hire Tom Cruise or Brad Pitt, with all their knowledge, experience and expertise in the film industry, plus an army of adoring fans to sell tickets to? It doesn't make any sense, does it?

The same is true in any field. The market will always prefer to work with the original, rather than an imitation, so you need to find your own alternative market instead, as this means that you have a better chance of finding some kind of gap you can actually fit into. Although this might need to be in a completely different industry, you will actually have a far greater chance of success.

4　Imitation Is No Competition!

When you imitate someone else you might *think* that you are setting yourself up as their direct competition and rival, but let's just unpack that theory. In order to be someone's competition you would first of all need to be at the same level as them professionally, academically and experientially, because otherwise how can you begin to offer something of the same calibre? It is highly unlikely that a company is going to hire someone who is *less* qualified, with less experience, to do the same job, for the same pay!

In addition, you would need to have the same status and social standing within the industry network, because your social value counts for a lot. There is truth to the saying *it's not what you know, it's who you know*. Most people would rather work with a friend who is part of the industry, who knows how that industry functions, than with a complete stranger who is new to it and still wet behind the ears. So imitating someone who is already established in the field isn't *actually* setting yourself up as competition – it's a silent admission of low self-esteem and a lack of personal direction.

5   It's A Distraction Technique

Speaking of personal direction, repeatedly trying to emulate the success of someone else is actually a subconscious distraction technique, because it pulls your focus away from discovering your own authentic path to success. While you are busy trying to copy what someone else has done, then you are not working on your own authentic goals and ambitions – you might not even know what they are, because you have been too busy trying to imitate another person's success. Imitation is one of the biggest blocks to manifestation, because you are aiming for something that isn't necessarily meant for you, while at the same time, ignoring your true destiny. This in turn leads to feelings of resentment and envy, which can hold you back even further.

If you have been unsuccessful in emulating another person's success and you have been trying to do so for several years, then take it as a sign that you are on the wrong path! Use the spell from earlier to let go of the dream and begin to embrace your true destiny instead, because that is where your success really lies, but you won't discover it until you stop trying to copy what everyone else is doing.

When Someone Is Trying to Steal Your Light

They say that imitation is the sincerest form of flattery. In small doses that may be true, but on-going imitation can be rather irritating. So what do you do if it's *your* success that people are trying to copy? This can be very frustrating. It's one thing knowing who your genuine competitors are, it's quite another when someone copies everything you do, allowing you to lay the groundwork so that they can try to hang onto your coat-tails and reap the same rewards, without having the relevant qualifications or experience. They are looking for an easy way to the top, because they don't want to have make the same effort you have made over the years.

It can be quite infuriating, but take comfort from the fact that if they feel the need to follow someone else, then they probably don't have what it takes to make a success of it, which is why they need to imitate *your* success instead. Authentic ambition blazes its own trail. It doesn't play *follow the leader!* That said, you are perfectly entitled to ring-fence and protect your own interests, using the following spell.

A Withering Spell to Protect Your Own Interests

A withering spell is a traditional practice witches use to wither away a negative influence or interference in their life. For this spell you will need a small apple, a carving tool such as an athame, garlic powder and a lidded jar big enough to contain the apple. An old candle jar works well.

On the night of the waning moon, carefully carve a keyword or two into the apple skin. So you could carve Shine-Stealer, Usurper or something similar. Hold the apple in your hands close to your chest and repeat this incantation three times to empower it to its purpose.

Those who try to steal my shine

Are now withering away

No longer will you cross the line

No more your game to play

What's mine is mine, I draw the line

I ring-fence my assets true

So go your own way from this day

Find the path that's meant for you.

Place the apple into the jar and sprinkle it liberally with the garlic powder, which is a natural banishing herb. Put the lid on the jar and keep it in a dark place, allowing the apple to wither away. This can take up to six months, until the apple has turned black and mouldy, so keep the spell jar in a garden shed or outside your front door. Once the apple has withered and is black and crumpled, you can throw it away or put it on the compost heap. The spell is complete and the usurper should have moved on to a new goal.

Imitation Vs Inspiration

Imitation should not be confused with inspiration. Inspiration is a gift and it is a vital part of any creative life and of manifestation. So what's the difference between the two? We all get inspired by others from time to time. For instance, you might see someone in a great outfit and it inspires you to buy some new clothes or get a new haircut. Or you might hear news of your sister's new job and it inspires you to try for a promotion at work.

Inspiration can come from many places, such as the things you see and hear, the things that are all around you. It hits you in the moment, like a flash in the pan, but rather than setting you on the path to immediate imitation, it is meant to evolve into something that is entirely personal to you.

It is possible to be over-inspired by someone or something, and this is what leads to imitation. If you find yourself copying everything that someone does, or wanting to own and do all the same things as them, then you have been overly-inspired and it is time to pull back. Consider what it is about this person that actually inspired you in the first place – how can you take the essence of that inspiration and re-fashion it to make it entirely your own?

Inspiration is meant to enhance your own pattern and individuality, to help you grow. It's not designed to turn you into a clone of someone else, which is the opposite of personal growth. That's how you stagnate and become fixated on having everything someone else has, rather than building an authentic life of your own. Be inspired by all means, but don't allow yourself to become over-inspired to the point of imitation. After all, you are not the moon – you hold your own light within, so you should have no need to steal the shine off someone else.

PART

12

MOON
DIVINATIONS

Divination is the art of seeing, commonly known as fortune-telling. It is one of the tricks of the witch's trade and most witches practice some aspect of it. Tarot cards are perhaps the most well-known divination tool, with oracle cards coming in at a close second. If you are interested in card readings, you might find my *Moon Magic* or *Celtic Magic* card decks useful. There are lots of other ways to practice divination too. Crystals, water, mirrors and pendulums are all tools used in foretelling the future and we will be looking at some of them in this chapter.

Dark Shadows

It is generally accepted that divination is a practice which should be performed after dark. Some witches refuse to do card readings or other divinations, until the sun has set, so it is an aspect of magical living that naturally aligns with the moon. Indeed, there is something very enchanting about setting up a crystal ball or scrying vessel in the dark, with a single candle flame and the moonlight being the only illumination. In the quiet reaches of the night, the unknown becomes known through the shadows reflected in the scrying vessel used.

However, any type of divination is always subject to change, so if you do not like what the crystal ball or whatever is showing you, then you have the option to change your patterns or your approach to life, in order to effect a different outcome. Nothing is set in stone and the future is always yours to create. Divination shows only what the most likely outcome is, given the current situation. If you alter the situation, then you alter your future too. The shadows of prophecy will shift and change shape, based on the decisions you make each day, so divination presents guidance only, rather than a set, unchangeable outcome.

Lunar Divination Tools

In this chapter, we will concentrate on the kind of divination tools which are linked to the moon, so crystals, mirrors, cards and bowls of water. While some crystal balls can be expensive, you do not need to spend a lot of money, for a simple bowl of water can be used in exactly the same way as a crystal ball.

Gazing into a vessel, be it water, mirror or crystal, in order to see images of the past, present or future, is known as scrying. Your scrying vessel should always be clean and dust free, or the water fresh and clear, to give a pure surface on which to scry. With any kind of scrying, visions can come in your mind's eye and this is more common to begin with. With greater practice you might start to see visions in the vessel itself. The first hint that a vision is about to appear in the vessel is when the surface suddenly seems to fill with cloud, or smoke. Maintain your concentration and when the clouds clear, the vision should play out in the vessel. This does take a lot of practice, so persevere.

◇ Crystal Balls: these represent the full moon and are attuned with the Mother aspect of the Triple Goddess. The ball should be a good size without being unwieldy. Traditionally it should fit easily into the palms of both hands, without being too heavy to hold. Ideally it should be placed on a stand, on a table laid with a black or dark-coloured cloth. This gives a shadowy background and ensures there are no gaudy patterns to interfere with the Sight.

◇ Water: this can be a natural body of water such as a loch or lake, but it is usually a bowl of water. Scrying bowls tend to be painted black inside to give a dark surface on which to scry. Water scrying uses the exact same process and techniques as scrying in a crystal ball, but because it is a more dynamic force, you might find that visions come to you more easily. For this reason, it is common practice to begin with water scrying, before moving onto crystal balls and dark mirrors.

◇ Dark Mirrors: a dark mirror, or scrying mirror, is a small mirror with a completely black surface. It could be made from a circle of black obsidian crystal, or it could be home made, with the sliver removed from a makeup mirror and the back painted black instead. You can even use a TV that is turned off as the black screen provides an instant scrying mirror! Dark scrying mirrors are probably the most difficult to master. They represent the dark moon and are attuned to the Crone. Some of them come as crystal balls too. Again, use the same techniques as with a crystal ball, but be aware that dark mirrors tend to take a bit longer to master.

Tips for A Successful Scrying Session

◇ Prepare the room by dimming the lights and lighting a single candle.

◇ Spread a black or dark-coloured cloth over a table.

◇ Place your chosen scrying vessel on the table and position yourself so that you can comfortably peer into it.

◇ Breathe slowly and evenly – don't hold your breath.

◇ Repeat a scrying chant such as the one given opposite.

◇ Concentrate on your question or query.

◇ Gaze into the centre of the vessel, with eyes that are softly focused. Blink when necessary.

◇ Note down any visions you had during your session, which should last no longer than 30 minutes, or you will tire your eyes.

Scrying Chant

It is common practice to begin a scrying session with a special chant.
This is a form of spoken intention and helps to set the tone of the
session. The chant can be said out loud or whispered under your breath.
You can make up your own chant or you can use this one.

Vessel deep shows visions true

Sights unseen betwixt me and you

What is unknown I now shall know

As through this vessel the visions flow

Secrets lost and truth revealed

Past, present and future now unsealed

So mote it be.

Are Magic Mirrors Real?

The concept of the magic mirror has been popularized over time by folklore and fairy-tales, most notably that of Snow White. There is some truth to the idea that a mirror can reflect visions, for that is what scrying is. It is about learning to see images of the past, present or future within the mirror, or other scrying vessel.

In the Far East, magic mirrors were quite common and their use dates back to approximately the 5th Century. These mirrors were usually made of highly polished bronze, with the backs being elaborately decorated. They were highly prized possessions and would be handed down from one generation to the next, as heirlooms. These mirrors were thought to reflect an unbiased view, offering insights into both good and bad tidings. Once again, this links back to the fairy-tale of Snow White and the magic mirrors of myth and legend, which can tell only the truth, regardless of whether the questioner will like it or not. Interestingly, magic mirrors were usually round or oval in shape, linking their power to that of the moon. Modern witches often have a round scrying mirror on their altar, or a round decorative mirror hung in their sacred space, to represent the moon and honour her energies.

Scrying mirrors are a more modern version of the Far Eastern magic mirror. They are most commonly made from black obsidian, such as the one said to have been used by John Dee, the famous astrologer to Queen Elizabeth I, which he called his *spirit mirror*, in reference to the fact that mirrors are said to be portals into the spirit realms and can reflect ghosts, spirits and glimpses into the fairy realm and Otherworld. For this reason, mirrors, scrying mirrors in particular, were often warded with protection magic to prevent any unwelcome guests passing through them as a portal. You will find a warding spell later on in this chapter.

How to Make a Dark Mirror

Moon Phase: make the mirror during a dark moon

Items required: a round picture frame about the size of a tea-plate, matt black paint and a paint brush, or black construction paper or card.

Although you can buy a dark mirror from new age stores and online, you can easily make your own. Take a circular picture frame to represent the moon and carefully remove the glass. Use the paint to cover the back of the glass and let it dry thoroughly. Add a second coat of paint and let this dry too. Alternatively, you could draw round the glass and cut a piece of black card to fit in the frame. Whichever method you choose, reassemble the picture frame with the black paint or card on the inside of the frame. This will keep the paint from scratching off or the card from ripping. You now have a dark mirror for your scrying sessions. Keep it on your lunar altar and use it for divination.

Protection Magic to Ward a Dark Mirror

To make sure that your scrying vessel is safe to use, you will need to protect it with a warding spell. First of all, cleanse the mirror by passing incense smoke all around it. You can use a smudge stick, an incense stick, or some of the Wish incense from the last chapter (page 124). Next sprinkle the mirror with a little sea salt, which acts as a blessing. Finally ward the mirror by dipping your finger into some Lunar Oil and trace a pentagram, or five-pointed star, on the back of the mirror as you say the following words of power.

No ill or bane this path shall seek

As visions true, the Scryer seeks

Visions come for highest good

I ward this mirror with a protective hood

So mote it be.

Developing Your Second Sight

Any type of divination can take time to master because it depends on your own personal level of psychic ability, or second sight, as it is sometimes known. Many people believe that you must be born with second sight, that it is a gift only a few people are blessed with. In fact, it is part of the survival instinct and we all have it within us. Your intuition is one of your most valuable assets. It is that part of you that instinctively has a good or bad feeling about a stranger you hardly know, or which prompts you to find an alternative route to work, only to discover later that there was heavy traffic or a road accident on your usual route.

We often credit animals with having great instincts, but the human instinct is no less finely tuned. Your intuition, or second sight, is a natural human ability. It works like a muscle, so the more you use it, the more it develops over time. Start to listen to your instincts more frequently. Pay attention to what they are trying to tell you and act upon this instinct. If you do, you will find that your insights from divination become much more profound. Use the following ritual to signal to your intuition that you are ready to listen, ready to *see* that which is otherwise unseen.

Lunar Charm for Second Sight

As you settle down to perform your divination practices, first of all light a white candle and say *I work in the light of all lights*. Next, close your eyes and breathe deeply three times. Picture the moon in your mind and now say:

Lunar Lady, Mother of dark and light

Open my mind's eye this night

As I see a dream within a dream

Reveal to me the realms of Unseen

Instincts strong and visions true

I welcome the Sight, as I learn from you.

When you feel ready, open your eyes and begin to scry or deal the cards. Enjoy your gift of second sight. Divination should not feel scary. You are simply tapping into your intuition in a magical way and intuition is a natural gift.

Lunar Stones for Divination

Moon Phase: put this divination tool together on the night of the full moon

Items required: a small pouch, lavender oil, tumble stones of the following crystals – clear quartz, snowy quartz, red jasper, moonstone, hematite.

First sprinkle the pouch, both inside and out, with a few drops of lavender oil. This will act as a cleansing agent to keep your crystals pure and free of negative energy. Each crystal represents a phase of the lunar cycle. Place them into the pouch and give them a shake. When you want to use them, shake the pouch three times as you ask your question, then draw out a single lunar crystal. Use the guide to interpret the answer to your question.

◇ Clear Quartz – represents the new moon, meaning new beginnings are under way but as yet unseen. The shoots are about to burst through, but on the surface everything looks dead and fallow. Have faith that things are being put into place for your highest good. You are surrounded by Maiden energy.

◇ Snowy Quartz – represents the waxing moon, meaning a time of fresh starts and planning is underway. Good things are coming to you and you are working hard to achieve your goals. You are surrounded by positive energy.

◇ Red Jasper – represents the full moon and the blood of the mother goddess. This is a vibrant time and you are reaping the rewards of your labour, however, it is not without difficulty or sacrifice. The end result will be worth the pain. You are surrounded by Mother energy.

◇ Moonstone – represents the waning moon, meaning that the hard work is done and a brief time of respite is to come. The cloudy aspect of this crystal means that you might not be able to see your way ahead right now, but trust that all will be well, given time.

◇ Hematite – represents the dark moon, meaning that you need to rest and recharge in preparation for the next cycle of growth and activity. Something may have been stripped from your life and you need to grieve the loss, or you may be experiencing a period of fatigue. Rest, recharge and recuperate at this time. New seeds are being sown in the darkness. You are surrounded by Crone energy.

Smoke On, Go!

Moon Phase: this is a good ritual for a waning or dark moon

Items required: a cauldron or heat proof bowl, sand, charcoal blocks, a lighter, dried herbs such as mugwort, white sage, basil and mint are good ones to use.

Smoke scrying is less well known than crystal or water scrying, but it can be very relaxing and beneficial for mental health. Make sure that you are outdoors or in a well ventilated room, away from any smoke detectors.

Fill the cauldron or bowl with sand to absorb the heat safely, then light a charcoal block and place it in the centre of the bowl. Next add the dried herbs to the charcoal block, a pinch at a time so that they burn slowly. The smoke will rise quite quickly, forming patterns in the air. Watch as these patterns unfold, making special note of any images you see such as hearts, arrows and other symbols. Use your intuition to interpret what these images mean for you. If the smoke is bringing the image towards you, that is a sign that it is coming your way, but if the smoke carries it away from you, then it is not meant to be, or will not happen for a long while. If the image travels straight up, the timing is as yet unclear. If the charcoal block goes out or the herbs don't burn, then it is not meant to be.

You can enhance your smoke scrying sessions by backlighting the smoke with a coloured light, such as a pink salt lamp. This gives the smoke added definition and makes it easier to scry out images and patterns.

Mother of Dark and Light

Moon Phase: make this stone at the time of the full moon

Items required: a round pebble or stone, black paint, white paint and two paint brushes, clear varnish

As you have seen throughout this book, the moon and the mother goddess she represents, is both light and dark, waxing and waning, Mother and Crone. We can tap into both these energies in divination.

Divination need not be complicated and sometimes all you need is a simple yes or no answer to a simple question. This is known as *binary divination*. The most popular binary divination tool is the pendulum, but you can also make a simple *binary stone* to achieve the same results. First find a pebble on the beach or the riverside. It should be roundish to represent the moon and it should feel nice in your hand. Take it home with you and paint one side white to represent the answer *Yes*. Allow the paint to dry, then turn the stone over and paint the other side black to represent the answer *No*. Wait for the paint to dry, before varnishing the entire stone to protect the paint. To use the stone, ask a simple binary question, then toss the stone in the air like you would a coin and see which side faces up when it lands. If the white side is facing upwards the answer to your question is yes, but if the black side is facing up the answer is no.

Cartomancy

Cartomancy is the art of using cards for insight, clarity and foresight – commonly known as fortune-telling or prophecy. As soon as playing cards were introduced in the 14th Century, people began to interpret them to mean certain things, for instance, the King or Queen of Hearts represented a new love interest, while the Jack of Hearts was someone to avoid! Likewise, the Ace of Spades was said to foretell a death in the family.

Each card held its own meaning, each suit represented something different. Hearts meant love and relationships, Clubs creativity and travel, Spades meant misfortune, warnings or conflict, while Diamonds heralded wealth and business ventures. The suits also corresponded to the four most common career paths of the Middle Ages, with the Hearts signifying the church, Spades the military, Clubs farming and agriculture and Diamonds merchants and business.

Over time, new card decks were introduced specifically for the purpose of divination, such as the Tarot deck. These decks have been both revered and feared at various points in history. There was a time when to be found in possession of a Tarot deck would most likely lead to a charge of witchcraft and possible hanging. However, these days we are safe to practice whatever kind of divination we choose, including cartomancy. If you want to use cards in your lunar divinations, then follow these simple tips to get the most out of your readings.

◇ Wait until sunset before performing a reading.

◇ Lay your cards on a plain, dark cloth so that the images are vibrant.

◇ Read your cards by candlelight or moonlight if possible.

◇ Cast your cards on the night of the full moon for the most prophetic results.

◇ Cleanse your cards with smoke on a waning moon.

◇ Bless your cards on a new to full moon by letting them sit in moonlight overnight.

◇ Try not to let anyone else handle your oracle cards – they should soak up your energy alone.

◇ Say a card blessing just before a reading, such as the one opposite.

Oracle Card Blessing Charm

As you shuffle the deck, repeat the following charm three times, then immediately deal the cards into your preferred spread. This will help to ensure the most accurate readings and an insightful session.

Card by card let the future unfold

Image by image a story is told

A pattern plays within this spread

For helpful insight, nothing to dread

For as the moon doth wax and wane

A question is posed, an answer is gained

Blessed be.

PART
13

SHADOW CRAFT

Natural magic isn't only about spellcraft, astrological signs and symbols or moon magic. It is also about the shadow craft in the darker reaches of the mind, the conscious and the unconscious and how they work together to create your reality. The light of the moon is mesmeric and meditative, sometimes full and bright, sometimes hidden by cloud, but always powerful. In the same way, the unconscious mind is always working away, although we are generally unaware of it. Programming the unconscious mind is a way of ensuring that your inner landscape remains positive and doesn't sabotage your chances of success. Likewise, you can tap into your unconscious mind, also known as the higher self, for guidance and self-support.

Finding Quiet Amid Chaos

The world can seem like quite a chaotic place at times and it can be difficult to keep that chaos from impacting your life and your mental well-being. However, being able to find a sense of calm and quiet amid this chaos is essential if you are to maintain peace of mind. Chaos, panic, fear and anxiety are all infectious, so it is vital that you learn to create your own boundary of mental peace and quiet. Think of the poem *If* by Rudyard Kipling and learn to *'keep your head when all about are losing theirs and blaming it on you'*!

Recognising the first stirrings of chaos is often half the battle. If you know that your workplace is stretched to breaking point at certain times, or you know that certain people carry drama with them like a torch of doom, then you can prepare yourself for the madness in advance. Sometimes though, chaos comes out of the blue. Accidents, illnesses and bereavements can all take us by surprise, bringing a certain amount of chaos with them, which is unavoidable. Try using this magical technique to find a space of calm and quiet when your environment turns frenzied.

Moonlight Shield Visualisation

Go to a quiet place and close your eyes. Breathe deeply three or four times. This will help to calm your nerves. Now in your mind's eye, visualize the full moon high in the sky, shining her light down on you. Feel the silvery rays on your skin and bathe in this imaginary light. In this way you are tapping into the lunar energies, even if its midday, through the power of visualization. Next imagine that the lunar rays form a shield of light all around you, sealing you in and keeping any negative chaos or drama at bay. Within this shield you are calm and peaceful, capable and strong. Once you can see yourself surrounded by a magical shield of moonlight, open your eyes, take three more deep breaths and go back out into the fray, knowing that you can handle the chaos by presenting the light of peace and calm.

Schedule Psychic Quiet Time

Lunar energies are quiet by nature. While the sun can be brash and obnoxious, the moon is gentle and subtle. The night time energies are ones which we often ignore, preferring the company of the family sitting around the TV on a dark night, to that of the stars and moon, but communing with the nightscape is a great way to enhance your psychic abilities and your natural instincts.

There is something magical about being awake when most people are fast asleep and the wee small hours of the night hold enchantment within them. The dark night encompasses the magical hours of storytelling – the witching hour of midnight, the devil's hour of 3am and the fairy hours of dusk and dawn. Try to schedule some psychic quiet time around these hours, perhaps going for a walk at dusk or dawn, or conducting a midnight scrying session or card reading. Perhaps you could do some star gazing during the devil's hour, in the safety of your garden or a friend's. Providing you are sensible and do not put yourself at risk, there is no reason why you cannot enjoy the nocturnal hours to your witchy heart's content. Enjoy the magic of the nightscape and commune with the moon.

The Witching Hour

The stroke of midnight is a liminal space between the end of one day and the start of the next. As such it is said to be infused with its own kind of magic. This magic is generally regarded as being positive and enchanting in nature. It heralds the beginning of the witching hour, which traditionally lasts until around 2am. It has often been linked to witches, fairies, prophetic dreams and visions. The witching hour is said to be an especially auspicious time for magic and spellcasting, so many modern witches use this time to add power to special rituals. Here are some tips for how you can make the most of this magical time of night.

◇ Take a ritual bath, steeped in Epsom, Dead Sea or Himalayan salts
◇ Perform a midnight divination
◇ Try astral projection exercises
◇ Write in your moon journal
◇ Work a dream incubation spell
◇ Cast a spell or ritual attuned with the moon phase
◇ Enjoy a midnight picnic with friends in a safe place, such as in your garden
◇ Cleanse your crystals and magical tools
◇ Do gentle bedtime yoga or some stretching exercises
◇ Meditate – you can use one of the guided meditations in this book or something else.

The Devil's Hour

The devil's hour is said to be around 3am. However, the term can also refer to any time after the midnight witching hour has passed and before the dawn chorus begins, so usually between 2am and 4am. In folklore, this is the time when hauntings are said to occur and ghostly spirits are believed to walk abroad at night. The devil's hour indicates a time when spooky things are more likely to happen. It is also a time when only those people who are working a nightshift (or those who are up to no good!) are out and about, as the rest of the world sleeps comfortably in their beds.

Most people have had the experience of waking suddenly in the middle of the night. The world is dark and quiet and you might wonder what it was that woke you from your slumber. This sudden jolt from sleep can mean that you wake in a panic, with your heart racing and your body drenched in a night sweat, especially if you were having a bad dream.

Waking up, into the silence that accompanies the darkest part of the night, can be quite unnerving. Everything is quiet; any noise you hear outside is automatically suspicious and any creaks coming from inside the house are easily attributed to ghostly goings-on. It's a spooky time of night and your imagination does its best to fill in the gaps, offering possible explanations of why you woke up in the first place – burglars, wildlife, ghosts?

The truth is that it is highly unlikely to be either ghosts or intruders that woke you, but something more mundane, such as an addiction, a drop in body temperature or a dip in your blood sugar levels. If you are a smoker for example, often it is the body's craving for nicotine that wakes you in the night. For non-smokers, the chill that accompanies a deep sleep, during which your body temperature drops, can be enough to bring you round temporarily, as you reach for an extra blanket or snuggle deeper under the covers. What if you wake up filled with dread, depression and dark thoughts? Well, scientists believe that this is most likely to be caused by a temporary drop in your blood sugar, which can cause low mood and melancholia. The remedy? Raise your sugar levels slightly by eating something sweet, such as a biscuit, a small piece of fruit or a small square of chocolate and you should find that you can drop off to sleep again more easily.

Moonstruck Melancholia

Sometimes the moon itself has a part to play in nocturnal low moods and night-time depression, because it helps the body to provide vitamin D. Although we often associate this vitamin with sunlight, because the moon *reflects* the sun's light, it too can boost your vitamin D levels. Sleeping with the blinds open can help to facilitate this. However, when the moon is waning or dark, it provides less light, meaning that your body converts less vitamin D as you sleep. This reduction in moonlight can have a similar affect to Seasonal Affective Disorder, which is where some people experience low mood during the darker months of autumn and winter, due to the lack of natural light.

During the latter half of the lunar cycle, when the moon wanes towards its darkest phase, you may experience an increase in night time depression and low mood in the evenings. This is a perfectly natural reaction to the lack of moonlight and its nothing to worry about. Usually it doesn't require any kind of medical intervention, as your mood will begin to lift again as the moon waxes towards full. It can, however, play havoc with your sleep patterns and circadian rhythm, leaving you over-tired, miserable and irritable. If this type of moon melancholia is something that you suffer from, then a simple remedy would be to take a vitamin D supplement during the time of the waning moon. You could also try eating more foods that are naturally rich in vitamin D, such as oily fish, eggs and red meat, during this phase of the lunar cycle. Also, try to get outside more during the day and make the most of the natural light that is available.

Moon Blues

Night time depression is a real issue for some people. They might feel okay during the day when they are busy and productive, but as soon as their head touches the pillow, intrusive thoughts kick in, leading to low mood, depression, bad dreams and sleepless nights. Sometimes it can seem as if all your worries are resting upon the pillow, just waiting to invade your mind and keep you awake at night.

Anyone can be affected by the moon blues, not just people who have a medical history of depression. This kind of low mood usually begins in the evening, as you wind down for the night. It creeps up on you bit by bit, until you feel sad and tearful by the time you go to bed. It is usually triggered by the quietness of the night, when you are not being distracted by screens or family responsibilities and there is nothing between you and your worries.

Pondering on the events of the day, worrying about the following day, mental stress, poor health, having too many responsibilities, financial anxiety and so on, can all trigger a bout of night-time depression.

We see this a lot in children who, as the evening wears on, with bedtime approaching, start to think about school the next day, gradually becoming quieter, less playful, more withdrawn, possibly even tearful. This is a classic sign that something is playing on their mind and all is not well. The same is true for adults too, but we frequently dismiss the symptoms.

So what can you do if you, or someone you know, is experiencing night-time depression? First of all, try to make the experience of winding down for the night as pleasurable as possible. Having a night time routine can be very comforting and reassuring, particularly if you are going through a difficult time or you have a stressful job. Play soft music that you only listen to at night, or make a playlist to which you can fall asleep. Invest in a white noise machine and listen to the soothing sounds of the sea, rainfall or crickets and frogs as you drop off to sleep. These are simple techniques that help to fill your mind with sound, rather than with worry or anxiety and so they help to keep troublesome thoughts at bay.

Try to make it a rule that you never go to bed without addressing your worries in some way first, whether that means talking them through with a loved one or writing them down in a journal. Do what you can to get your concerns out in the open, so that they have less power to ambush you from your pillow in the middle of the night!

Meditation

Meditation is another great way to attune with the inner reaches of the mind and that which is hidden. Just like the moon, your higher self is always there, but you may not always listen to its wisdom, so meditating gives your higher self a chance to communicate with your conscious mind. In meditation you are inviting your subconscious to take centre stage for a time, to offer advice, encouragement and guidance. It has many benefits, both mentally and physically. Spending time in meditation can help you to relax, it reduces levels of stress and anxiety, it can alleviate feelings of irritability or restlessness. Meditation is also good for increasing your sense of self-awareness and emotional intelligence, plus it has the added benefit of developing your patience and sense of control over your emotions.

Building a meditative exercise into your magical practice is a fantastic way to learn about visions, pre-cognition and prophecy, dream worlds and other realms, the meaning of signs and symbols etc. In addition, it helps to develop your visualization skills, and in turn your ability to envision and manifest a better future for yourself, so there are really no reasons not to give it a try! Guided meditations, such as the one below, are often the best to begin with because, as the name suggests, they take you on a mental journey, guiding you through an imaginary realm before bringing you back to the current moment in time. A guided meditation, also known as a path-working, is a bit like mindfulness but with storytelling attached! Try the path-working on page 167 and see what it brings up for you.

Persephone's Labyrinth of the Dark Moth

For this guided meditation it is useful to have someone read it out loud to you, or alternatively, you can record it in advance so that you can play it back whenever you want. Lay down in a comfortable position and close your eyes. Breathe deeply for a while, until you start to feel nicely relaxed, then proceed to visualize the guided meditation below.

You find yourself standing on a forest path. The night air is bracing and chill. The moon above is bright and full, lighting your way. You set off walking through the woods. In the distance you hear a soft voice whispering your name. It sounds as if the dry autumn leaves are calling out to you. You follow the path through the woods until you come to a moss-covered cave.

A lady stands at the mouth of the cave, wearing a flowing gown in the dark colours of autumn; mulberry, grey, bronze and deep purple. A lacy network of cobwebs is draped over the fabric, bejewelled with dewdrops that glimmer in the moonlight and a sweeping train falls from the gown, made up of dry autumn leaves. Her hair falls in a dark curtain, almost to her knees and her dark eyes have a glint of amber gold within them. She is Persephone, Lady of the Underworld, Mistress of Shadows and Spirits. She beckons you to follow her and you walk behind her down a steep path, tangled with tree roots and overhung with boughs of fir trees, until you find yourself in a grove of trees and at the beginning of a labyrinth.

"Welcome to my dark labyrinth, Shadow Weaver. Shall we venture into its centre to see who awaits?" You nod your head and follow Persephone as she leads you along the winding path of the labyrinth. As she walks, she begins to chant and you join in with her song.

Ever circling, ever turning, take me to the centre;

Ever constant, every changing, moving to the centre.

After a time, you find yourself in the very centre of the labyrinth, where a stone pillar supports a beautiful ornate lantern. Persephone moves to the lantern, lights the candle within, and says;

"At the centre of all things is the light of all lights, the light of Spirit and the light of hope, reflecting the promise of the moon above"

The ornate knot-work of the lantern casts dancing shadows around the labyrinth. The fir trees sway in the breeze, seeming to dance in the candlelight. A tiny black moth flies out of the darkness to the light of the lantern. Again and again, the little moth flies against the lantern and you watch in fascination until, in a single quick movement, Persephone reaches out and gently catches the moth. It sits peacefully in her hand and you take a closer look at its beautiful dark markings.

"Light any spark in the dark and the moth will come, for he is eternally drawn to the deeper darkness beyond the flame. As he struggles to reach the shadow-side of candlelight, he exerts himself, constantly striving to reach his dark goal, until he is his own undoing. For, of course, it is an illusion and the moth will never attain the deeper darkness, except in his own demise.

"Human nature is very similar. You have a tendency to believe that circumstances are somewhat blacker and darker than they really are, so you do not see the light. You forget to respect its heat and warmth, so you become burned by sorrow. Remember that in the darkest of times, the light is always there, if you only look for it." Persephone blows gently on the moth and it flies away into the night, unscathed by its brush with fire.

"Go now, Shadow Weaver, and walk the labyrinth back to your own realm." You leave Persephone in the middle of the labyrinth and take the circling path back out into the woods. Eventually you see the cave and the path back to the world of consciousness. When you feel ready, open your eyes and become aware of your surroundings. Write down your mediation experiences, and how Persephone's words have resonated with you, in your moon journal, then go about your day.

Moon Journal

If you haven't started a moon journal yet, then I urge you to do so. Traditionally magical journals are handwritten, but you can start a digital one if you prefer, or add a moon magic section to your current Book of Shadows if you have one. Use the moon journal to keep a track of your meditations, spells, rituals, manifestations and so on. It is also wise to make a note of how the moon affects your moods and behaviours as she moves through her cycle. Do you feel most powerful at the full moon during the time of the Mother, or during a waning or dark moon during the time of the Crone? How does a new moon make you feel; optimistic, nervous, restless? Keeping a moon journal will reinforce your connection to lunar energies and you can record your most successful rituals, so that you can repeat the patterns that work for you. Remember that all magic is a personal journey and your path is a unique one which only you are destined to tread. Here are some tips for what to add to your moon journal:

◇ Favourite crystals and the lunar energies they work best with

◇ The moon cycle and how it reflects in your moods

◇ Herbs and night flowering blooms you can use in lunar spells

◇ Your dreams and how they alter throughout the moon's phases

◇ Your patterns of concentration – does the moon have an impact?

◇ Favourite spells and rituals for attuning with the moon

◇ Lunar deities and their attributes

◇ Lunar totems you would like to work with in ritual

◇ Different moon names from different cultures, or devise your own

◇ Esbat rituals and traditions

PART
14

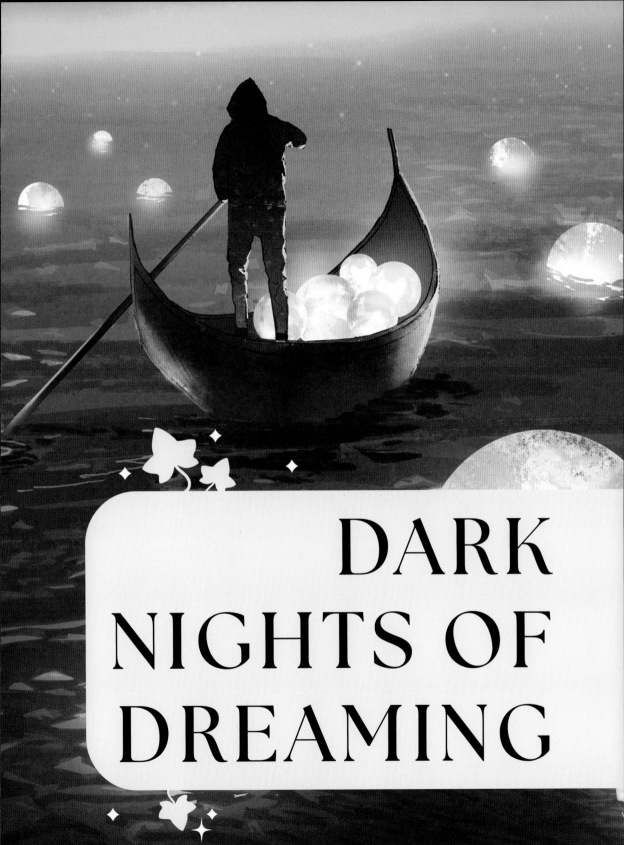

DARK NIGHTS OF DREAMING

Your dreams are far more than rambles through night-time realms of wonder and imagination. They are a way to process life events, work through your emotions, face fears and even find solutions to problems. Everyone dreams. It is a natural part of your nightly sleeping pattern. However, you may not always remember your dreams. Sometimes they fade almost as soon as you have opened your eyes, while at other times the dream is so vivid it stays with you for the rest of the day.

Many people believe that the moon has a profound effect on their dreams and their sleeping patterns in general. It is not uncommon to have a more restless night and more vivid dreams during a full moon, for instance. This could be because the night sky is much brighter, making a deep, dreamless sleep more difficult.

You might also see the moon in your dreams as well, with different lunar phases thought to signify different things. Dreaming of a new moon could mean that a fresh challenge is on the way, while a full moon denotes success. Dreaming of a waning or dark moon, or the moon hidden by mist or cloud, is thought to represent something which is hidden or repressed weighing on your mind. Dreaming is a magical experience in its own right. In your dreams you can fly, have super-powers, win the lottery or meet your idols. There are no limits. A whole world of possibility is open to you as you slumber. You will spend approximately one third of your life asleep, so with all this going on, it makes sense to try and harness such power or, at the very least, understand it a little better.

And So to Bed...

Creating a peaceful night-time routine is the first step in harnessing your nocturnal visions. You need to feel safe, warm and comfortable in order to have a good night's sleep. You should also be as relaxed as possible and for this purpose, lavender is your best friend. Begin your night routine with a lavender-scented bath or shower. There are hundreds of lavender-based bath and body products on the market for all budgets, so you should be able to find something you like. Next open the bedroom window slightly to allow the night air to circulate and draw the blinds if you wish, or leave them open to the moon's rays.

Ensure that your bed is as comfy as you can make it, without it being stifling. The idea is to cocoon yourself in soft nightwear and bedclothes. Scent your bedding with a lavender pillow spray or a few drops of lavender oil. You could also burn a lavender-scented candle for half an hour before you turn out the light and go to sleep. Grab a relaxing drink such as hot chocolate or a special cup of night-time tea, and curl up under the duvet with a good book. Sip your tea and read until you feel drowsy, then blow out the candles, turn off the lights and sleep, perchance to dream.

The Psychology of Sleeping Positions

Your preferred sleeping position says a lot about your state of mind and psychologists have come up with interesting interpretations for each posture. While we move through many positions each night, the one that you habitually adopt is your natural preference.

◇ Foetal – curled up, with knees brought up to the chest and arms tucked in. This is the position of the babe in the womb and is the most common sleeping position. Both children and adults adopt this pose. It indicates a fairly relaxed person, though it can also relate to shyness and timidity. Interestingly, it is often the position adopted by someone who is going through a trauma of some kind, reflecting their inner feelings of insecurity and the need to curl up and protect themselves. People often adopt this position when they need to have a good cry.

◇ Log – sleeping on the side, legs and arms straight down. This denotes a fairly balanced individual, one who is open to others and quite sociable. However, there is also a total lack of defence in this position which means that it can be easy to take advantage of this person.

◇ Yearning – another side position, but this time the sleeper might have one leg slightly bent as if stepping forward. Also the arms tend to be reaching out away from the body, as if trying to hold onto something. This is perhaps the most vulnerable of the poses, indicating a fragile personality who has in all likelihood experienced trauma of some kind. The outstretched arms could just as easily be used for defence though and this denotes a lack of trust in others and a willingness to stand up for themselves.

◇ Soldier – flat on the back, legs slightly apart, arms relaxed by the side. This is the pose of complete confidence! This sunbathing position indicates someone with a strong sense of self, one who is comfortable being the centre of attention. They know who they are and what they want from life and they are ready to go out and get it. However, the soldier is always on high alert and this individual might have trouble truly relaxing and letting go of control.

◇ Freefall – flat on the stomach, face turned to one side, arms bent at the elbows with the hands raised. This is the position of someone who is completely closed off from others. It is a pose of self-protection, as all the vital organs are tucked in close to the mattress and the heart is turned away, as the sleeper presents their back to the room. This denotes someone who is suspicious and who does not trust or open up to other people very easily.

◇ Starfish – flat on the back, arms and legs spread wide, reaching towards the four corners of the mattress and taking up as much space as possible. This denotes someone who is always ready to help other people. They are ready to leap into action at a moment's notice and enjoy being of service to others, yet it can lead to a martyr mind-set or over extending oneself if not carefully monitored.

Types of Dreams

There are various types of dreams, from those that recur over and over again, to the terror of the nightmare. Most of us experience a wide variety of dreams, often experiencing two or three types within the same night. Keeping a record can help you to identify the kind of dreams you have and how the moon might be affecting them. Lots of people like to write down their dreams as soon as they wake up, keeping a note pad and pen by the bed for this purpose. You could also make a voice note on your phone.

Whatever way you choose to record your dreams it is highly likely that they will fall into one of the following categories.

◇ Precognitive Dreams – usually these are visions of something which has yet to happen, also known as annunciation dreams. You might dream that you have a baby then discover that you are pregnant, or you might dream that you get your ideal job etc.

◇ Lucid Dreams – this is when you have the sudden realisation within the dream that you are in fact dreaming and it is not real. Often people wake up shortly after becoming lucid in their dreams, but if you can manage to remain asleep, sometimes you can take control of the dream and direct it like a movie. This takes practice though.

◇ Incubated Dreams – this is when you have asked for a very specific dream to come to you, perhaps for guidance or answers to a problem.

◇ Recurring Dreams – dreaming of the same thing over and over again. Pay special attention to these dreams as they are usually a message from your higher self. Once you act upon the message, the dreams will stop.

◇ Visitation Dreams – dreaming of the dead. These dreams often happen on special anniversaries such as birthdays or the anniversary of the death. They bring comfort and guidance and should not be discounted as imagination. Waking up can be tough though, as the loss is felt once more.

◇ Nightmares – also known as night terrors, these dreams urge us to face our fears. Common nightmares which we all have include being chased or hunted, falling from a great height, being naked in public, being laughed at on stage, crashing a car or plane, drowning, and failing some kind of exam or test.

Dreaming of a Past Life

In addition to the types of dreams above, you might also experience dreams that show a life you lived before, in a different incarnation. In these past life dreams you are likely to have a completely different appearance which becomes apparent only when you do something mundane in the dream, such as look in a mirror or brush out your hair. Such dreams might be accompanied by a feeling of déjà vu or a sense of knowing that you are seeing visions of the past. People might call you by a different name, or you will be surrounded by faces you don't know but feel connected to. Often you and those around you will be wearing clothes from a different time period. It is also not unusual in these dreams to see how you died. It might feel brutal at the time, but check your birth marks when you wake up, as these are said to be leftover traumatic injuries from past lives. Do you have a birth mark that matches with an injury or death blow from the past life dream? If so, it could be your soul's way of reminding you that you have many lifetimes of experience and wisdom to draw upon.

Dreamweaver

Dream incubation is the practice of requesting that a particular type of dream come to you within the next few nights. There are many reasons why you might decide to do this. It could be that you wish to connect with your ancestors or a deceased loved one via a visitation dream, or you want to experience a past life dream or a lucid dream that you can control. Whatever your reasons, sleeping on an issue can be hugely beneficial, so try this ritual and see what turns up in the night, as you allow your dreams to tell you a bedtime story.

How to Incubate a Dream

To begin, think about the kind of dream you want to have and write it down on a piece of paper. You might put something like *I wish to meet my deceased grandmother in dreams because I miss talking to her.* Once you have the intention of the dream written down, add a drop of lavender essential oil to the paper, then fold it and place it within your pillow case. Sprinkle a drop or two of the oil onto the pillow case, lay down and relax. Whisper what you want to dream about into your pillow as you fall asleep. This might not work immediately, but within the next seven nights, the dream you requested should manifest itself. Just be sure to write it down when you wake up!

Riding the Nightmare

Nightmares or night terrors are a type of intrusive thought. These disturbing visions can have an adverse effect on your mental, emotional and physical health, especially if they happen frequently. In order to begin taming the 'night mare' we need to understand where she comes from.

In folklore, the night mare was a spirit horse often associated with the equine goddesses Epona or Rhiannon, as well as the Kelpie of Celtic legend. The Kelpie was a fairy horse that would graze by the side of a loch, waiting for an unsuspecting human to come along. Initially it would be friendly, allowing itself to be petted, but as soon as it was mounted or bridled, the kelpie was said to gallop back into the depths of the loch, drowning its rider in the process. Interestingly, the element of water is linked to dreams, intuition and emotion, so it makes sense that the kelpie, with its lethal dash into the water, is a version of the night mare.

Perhaps the most famous night mare of all is the one depicted in Henry Fuseli's 1781 painting The Nightmare, which shows a fearsome horse's head peaking thorough the bed-curtains at a sleeping woman. Accompanying the horse in his observation of the sleeper is a small demon squatting on her chest. This relates to the sensation of feeling a weight pressing down on the chest that some people experience during a bad dream. Often this sensation is caused by stress, indigestion or respiratory issues, yet the 18th-century notion that it was caused by the presence of a demon has become a common, if rather romantic, aspect of dream lore.

Another indication of the night mare's presence in your dreams is that of sleep paralysis, which is when your mind wakes up moments before your body receives the message that it is time to awaken. This effectively means that although you are semi-conscious, you can't move your body for a few seconds after waking, leading to feelings of panic until the paralysis passes and you can move again. People also report sensing a presence in the room with them when they experience sleep paralysis, which further increases their unease and terror. This can happen as you transition from waking to sleeping, and vice versa.

Although sleep paralysis happens when you are semi-conscious, either as you begin to drop off to sleep or when you wake up, it is still considered to be a form of night terror and a sleep disorder. However, it is a natural phenomenon, because it is caused by the body being programmed to lie still when in a deep sleep so as to protect itself from injury.

Back in Henry Fuseli's time though, none of this would have been common knowledge and sleep disorders would have been explained by tales of demons and phantom horses sent in the night to spirit you away as you slept. Thus the 'night mare' was created.

Shades, Shadows and Dark Man Dreams

Sensing a presence in the bedroom during your sleep is often the most disturbing sleep disorder you can ever experience, especially when you open your eyes and see a shadowy figure standing in the corner or, worse, leaning over you as you slumber! Sleepers sometimes experience the sensation of having the breath sucked out of them by these shades and they may wake up coughing or gasping for breath. Such nocturnal visions can be quite terrifying, especially when they bleed into the first waking moments of reality, but they are also fairly common. People from all over the world, from all different cultures, have reported having such dreams, so where do these visions and hallucinations come from?

The figures we see in our dreams usually relate to people we know, or those we wish we knew. Dreaming of a famous singer or actor would be a typical wish-fulfilment dream, while dreaming of your old teacher might indicate that you are feeling more studious or have recently accomplished something that you are proud of.

Night-time visits from shades and shadowy figures, however, are much less congenial and each one is slightly different in nature. A shade is usually a coalescence of dark energy and may appear as an insubstantial shadow with no defined shape. If this kind of apparition is disturbing your sleep, then clear away the dark energy by cleansing your bedroom with incense or a smudge stick.

Do this during a waning moon, moving in an anti-clockwise direction, to draw the dark energy away from you.

A shadowy figure is rather more sinister and usually has the appearance of a tall man, hence why these nightmares are sometimes referred to as *dark man dreams*. Often this figure is a simple humanoid shape, but sometimes he can be much more defined, with specific items of recognizable clothing, such as a hat. The dark man has even made his way into popular culture via TV shows such as *Ghost Whisperer* and the iconic horror film franchise *Nightmare on Elm Street*, where Freddy Krueger is the sinister hat-man of your worst nightmares! These pop-culture images then feed back into your psyche, leading to more dark man dreams, so it can be something of a vicious cycle.

Psychologically, dark man dreams come from the hidden reaches of the subconscious mind. They symbolize deep and disturbing repressed memories, intrusive, sometimes violent thoughts and your deepest fears personified. If you have a history of being abused, then these dreams can be especially disturbing. In general, though, dark man dreams are a sign of high anxiety levels that do not abate during sleep. Having such visions indicate that you are feeling overwhelmed, vulnerable and out of control.

In some cases, the shadowy figure could also be a warning against trusting the wrong person, particularly if you have recently met someone who you are not sure about – take this dream as a sign from your higher self that it is safer to keep away from that person. As the name suggests, dark man dreams are harbingers of sinister intention and could indicate that someone is a threat to your safety, or that potential danger is on the cards. Heed the warning, thank the shadowy figure for the heads-up, and remember that darkness is dispelled by light, so do things to increase the light in your life and in your heart. Seek out counselling if you need it, address old issues, heal old wounds, take a holiday to de-stress and surround yourself with a circle of protective light. Once you have acted upon his warning, the dark man should trouble your sleep no more.

Nocturnal Flashbacks

Bad dreams can also come about due to illness and mental health issues such as depression, anxiety and most especially Post Traumatic Stress Disorder (PTSD) and Complex Post Traumatic Stress Disorder (CPTSD). When someone has been traumatized, often the easiest way for the psyche to deal with traumatic memories, or even just repressed and half-forgotten memories, is during sleep. While amnesia might cloud a person's waking mind, in sleep they are relaxed and therefore better able to receive messages from the subconscious. In this sense, difficult memories can be addressed in the dream state, via nocturnal flashbacks.

Often we imagine flashbacks to be very dramatic experiences, and sometimes they are, but they can also be quite subtle too, creeping up on you when you least expect it. This is what nocturnal flashbacks are like, and although they can still *feel* like nightmares depending on what the flashback is about, they are, in fact, memories. Like all flashbacks, they are completely involuntary and you have no control over them – it's not just a case of reminiscing. When you experience a flashback in your sleep, it is all too easy to dismiss it as simply a bad dream or a rough night, but it is only by paying attention to the visons that they will stop.

Nocturnal flashbacks are a polite way for old fragmented memories to knock on the door of your conscious mind. In short, they want to know if you are ready to handle them in your waking life, so they drop into your dreams to see what you will do with them. Often, these visions then begin to bleed into your waking life more gradually, eventually leading to actual flashbacks during the day, or to a steady drip-feed of additional memories related to the dreams, coming to the surface at random hours of the day, leading you to wonder if you are just day-dreaming or losing your wits!

Recurring nocturnal flashbacks can be quite unsettling, especially if they relate to your trauma. A soldier dreaming of being back in the theatre of war for instance, is basically being re-traumatized on a nightly basis and such dreams will only abate when the initial battle trauma is being actively addressed, usually through an intense period of counselling.

Coping with such dreams can be extremely difficult and means that you are not getting the rest that you need in order to recover. This is because the nocturnal flashbacks effectively mean that you remain stuck in the realms of your trauma, rather than being free to move on with your life. So how do you know if you are having a standard nightmare, or a more intense nocturnal flashback? Well, if you can relate to three or more of the indicators opposite, you might be experiencing nocturnal flashbacks.

Indicators of Nocturnal Flashbacks

Not all bad dreams are the stuff of nightmares. Some are made from fragmented memories, emotions and physical cues that come from a specific event in your past and they are designed to help you come to terms with old trauma. Common indicators of this include the following and could be a sign that you would benefit from seeking medical help or counselling.

◇ The dream feels more like a memory, it feels real
◇ You experience the dream in all of your senses through sight, sound, smell, taste and touch
◇ It feels like you are living the dream, rather than dreaming the dream
◇ The dream is recurring and repetitive
◇ The dream never changes – it's the same thing over and over
◇ You cry in your sleep, waking up in tears, on a damp pillow
◇ You scream in your sleep, waking yourself or others during the night
◇ You act out the dream in your sleep – walking, crawling, fighting etc.
◇ You feel helpless within the dream or to stop the dream from happening
◇ You dread going to sleep because you fear the dream is waiting for you
◇ You feel intense panic, waking up fighting or thrashing around
◇ You have considered self-medicating with drugs or alcohol to induce a dreamless sleep
◇ You avoid sleep as much as possible
◇ You can relate the dream directly to an event or period in your own life

A Ritual to Come to Terms with Flashbacks

Flashbacks can be very debilitating, but believe it or not, they are actually a sign of healing. When your mind throws up memories in the form of a flashback, it is actually processing the events of the past. Often one's instinct is to try to avoid triggering flashbacks as much as possible, however, inviting them in is often a better way of handling them. While this might seem counter-intuitive, when you invite the flashbacks to come to you, you are actually taking charge of how and when the memories come through, by giving them a designated time and space. To do this, find a quiet space where you will not be disturbed, but try to make sure there is someone within calling distance, even if only on the phone. Next light a white candle and say the following words;

A burning flame within my mind

Hidden deep, it keeps me blind

I bring it forth into the light

The past now present, within my sight

Teach me, tell me, show me more

Flashback to a time before

In the present I'm safe and sound

To heal within, the trauma unbound.

Sit or lay in a comfortable position and allow your mind to go where it will. Now that you have given your mind permission to show you the things it wants you to know, you can begin to process the past, one flashback at a time. The flashbacks might come instantly, or you might doze off and experience them in your sleep. They might also come later that day or night. As soon as they have passed, take the time to write them down in your Moon Journal, pinning the trauma down on the page where it can do you no harm. Repeat this ritual as often as you need to and give your mind permission to speak. Once your subconscious mind feels seen and heard, it is likely that the flashbacks will begin to recede a little.

Twilight Dreams

Certain dreams are so common that almost everyone will experience them at one time or another. Dreams have long been considered a means of gathering information and insight as we sleep. They are a great way for your higher self to communicate with you, and also for spirits guides, angels, deceased loved ones and other messengers to pass on information too. Here are some of the most common dreams and their possible meanings.

Being Chased or Hunted Down

The atmosphere of this dream can be either playful or sinister. If you dream that you are a child again, playing chasing games with friends and siblings, this would indicate that you need to get in touch with your inner child and become more playful in your daily life.

Being chased by a lover in a playful *kiss-chase* kind of way could also indicate that you need to bring a more playful attitude to your relationship, or that you are so fond of the chase you never allow yourself to be truly caught in a committed relationship.

Dreaming that you are being chased by the police or some other figure of authority indicates a guilty conscience. What have you done, or are contemplating doing, that goes against your own moral values or the rules of society? Heed the warning of this dream and keep your nose clean, because you're likely to get caught!

Chasing dreams can quickly turn into nightmares, so if you dream that you are being hunted down by someone who means you harm, this would indicate that you feel vulnerable or threatened in some way. It could also mean that someone is a threat to you in real life, particularly if you have been experiencing dark man dreams too. Think back over the dream – do you recognise the person hunting you, or is it an unknown assailant? Either way, take extra precautions in your daily life and become more aware of how much information you give away to strangers. Not everyone you meet will be trustworthy, so take care how much trust you place in others.

Crash and Burn

Dreaming that you are in a vehicle that crashes is very common. Cars and planes are the usual mode of transport in these dreams, but it could also be a boat, a train, even an elevator. In these dreams you are in some kind of moving vehicle that suddenly crashes, then bursts into flames or sinks into deep water. This classic dream signifies a feeling of being out of control and suffering the consequences. It can also highlight driver anxiety, or apprehension regarding an upcoming trip or holiday.

If the vehicle bursts into flames upon impact of the crash, this means that you are in the midst of strong, feisty or passionate emotions. This is especially the case if you were the one driving the vehicle, while to watch a vehicle crash and burn in front of you, symbolizes that you could be burnt by the emotions of someone else, someone who draws you into a situation against your better judgement, say, for example, a romantic affair. To watch another vehicle crash and burn behind you, say in the rear view mirror of the car you're driving, indicates that you have had a lucky escape from a situation that would have been harmful or which would have caused you pain.

Crashing into deep water is a sign that not only do you fear a loss of control, but that you are also feeling quite overwhelmed by deep emotions too. If you can escape the vehicle and swim to safety, then all should be well, but if you remain trapped inside, or you find that you cannot swim away for whatever reason, then this is a sign that you need to reassess your life and how much responsibility you take on board. Don't agree to everything you are asked to do and then feel like you've lost control of your life and you're drowning as a result.

Humiliation

Humiliation dreams come in several guises, including dreaming that you are naked in public, that you lose your notes when you're about to give a speech, or your voice when you're about to sing or act on stage, or that people are pointing at you and laughing for some reason. In short there is no end to the number of ways in which your dreams can humiliate you! Generally, this kind of dream comes about when you are feeling low in self-esteem or when your confidence has been knocked in some way. Perhaps you have failed an exam, lost your job, or you've just been dumped by your partner, or you've discovered that someone you trusted has deceived you and you feel stupid because of their betrayal. Whatever it may be, this dream is a reflection of that reality. It comes to highlight the humiliation you are feeling and to warn you not to let your confidence plummet any further. Now is the time to start picking yourself back up again.

Flying and Falling

Having dreams that you can fly is a sign of high ambition and future success. This is the case whether you are piloting a plane or flying with a superpower or a magic cape. However, the first indicates that your success will come via external power and support from others, while the second indicates that success will come via your own inner talents and gifts. Flying dreams can be very pleasant, offering the dreamer a chance to look down on their familiar world from a totally different perspective. This perspective can last well beyond the moment you wake up, particularly if you fly away to escape a problem in the dream, as it is likely that you will rise above your troubles in reality too.

To dream that you're falling is a sign that something is about to pull you down to earth with a bump. It could signify a disappointment up ahead, or a failure of some kind. How you fall determines the severity of the disappointment, so if you fall fast and hard, tumbling uncontrollably, then the disappointment will be significant. If, however you float down more gently, then the disappointment will be a temporary set-back. If you dream that someone pushes you from a height, which results in the fall, take this as a sign that someone is trying to tear you down or undermine you in real life. Heed the warning and do what you can to protect your own interests.

Often, flying and falling dreams come about during short periods of astral projection, which is when the astral self, floats up and away from the physical body for a short time during sleep. We will be looking at astral projection later in the book, but for now know that when you wake up with a start after dreaming that you're flying or falling, this could be a sign that you have been astral travelling during your sleep.

Wish Comes True

There are many different kinds of wish-fulfillment dreams, but they usually involve receiving some kind of extravagant gift, such as a fancy sports car, a race horse or a financial windfall. If you dream that have won the lottery, get a full house at the bingo hall, or that you are crowned Miss World or something similar, this type of wish-fulfillment dream is a hint as to what you yearn for. Pay attention, because the dream could also contain clues as to how you can make this wish a more realistic goal and something that you can actively work towards achieving.

Sex Idol

Having sexy dreams about someone is another type of wish-fulfillment dream. Usually you dream of someone that you have a crush on but who is beyond your reach in reality, so actors, singers and other famous people. These dreams are great fun to experience and they can put a spring in your step and a smile on your face for the rest of the day. They can also indicate that you might be feeling neglected, or demonstrate a lack of passion, romance and intimacy in your life. Furthermore, these dreams can stay with you for a long time afterwards, making you smile each time you remember them. So next time you wake up after dreaming about your idol, keep your eyes closed, go back to sleep and enjoy it while it lasts!

A Pouch for Sweet Dreams

Magic can be time-consuming, but at some point amid all your moon rituals you will need to sleep. You can't stay up casting spells all night, every night! So here is a little charm bag to ensure that you enjoy sweet dreams when you go to bed. Take a small pouch and place inside it the following crystals: moon stone for dreaming; amethyst for protection; rose quartz for love; and obsidian to represent night-time. Next add the following dried herbs: lavender for deep sleep; camomile for calm; and mugwort for prophetic visions. Give the pouch a good shake to mix up the contents and place it in the light of the moon for one full lunar month, new moon to new moon. Then place it under your mattress or hang it from a bedpost to work its magic and fill your nocturnal mind with the sweetest dreams. Remember that bedtime can be a magical experience as well as a relaxing one. Sweet dreams!

PART

15

ANIMAL ALLIES

Some creatures have long been linked with magic and the moon. Cats, wolves, owls, hares and so on are all thought to have a special connection with the lunar cycle. In magic, witches often call upon the attributes of particular animals for certain spells or needs. So you might call upon the spirit of the cat for greater autonomy for instance, or the wolf for team building. This is known as invoking the spirit of the animal and it is easily done.

Invoking Your Power Animal

You can light candles if you wish, but they are not necessary. Invoking a power animal can be as simple as closing your eyes and asking that animal spirit to guide and protect you. Alternatively, you could wear a charm or bring images and ornaments that represent your chosen power animal into your home. Here are a few of the most well-known lunar power animals.

Wolves

The image of a lone wolf howling at the moon is an iconic one. Howling is how wolves communicate and, like most hunter animals, they like to take advantage of the bright night on a full moon. They also howl to find a mate, making their presence known by scenting an area and then howling to draw attention to themselves.

Wolves have no natural predator, which means that technically they are at the top of the food chain – humans require guns and traps to defeat them and so we have usurped their place. Wolves are now a protected species in some parts of the world and, although sadly they are extinct in Britain, their numbers are gradually increasing in parts of Europe. They have been unfairly demonized in popular culture, as have witches, so it should come as no surprise that many witches like to work with the spirit of the wolf as a spirit animal. They are resilient, brave, loyal and great survivalists. The old saying *the wolf is at the door* refers to a time of hardship and poverty, indicating that one needs to be strategic in survival, just as a wolf would be. As a power animal you can call on the wolf for all issues of courage, courting, family, team building, hunting out a good deal or creative survival strategies to get you through the lean times.

Cats

If you have ever tried to keep a cat indoors on the night of the full moon you will know how difficult it is! These little hunters love the moonlight and enjoy their night-time revels. Even house cats tend to act differently during a full moon, often being more playful as they 'hunt' their toys. The cat is probably the best known witch's familiar too, and they do tend to take an interest in magic. They might flip your tarot cards, grab at your pendulum or stare into the flame of a fire or candle.

We can learn a lot from cats. They are such autonomous creatures, often spending their time with neighbours so that no-one ever truly 'owns' them. They seem fearless, traversing the neighbourhood at night without a care in the world. They do what they want, when they want and they don't care what anyone else thinks of them. Cats have great confidence and they are not afraid to defend themselves when they have to. As a power animal, the spirit of the cat can help you to become more confident, independent, fearless and free-thinking.

Stags and Deer

As creatures of Artemis, stags and deer are inextricably linked with the moon and the hunt. They are prey animals, so they tend to be very highly strung and easily spooked by loud noises and the unexpected. Although their instinct is to herd together, in the autumn the stag rut takes place, so you may come across a lone stag during this time of year, as he is looking for rival stags to fight. They are formidable opponents, yet they can be surprisingly gentle with people, so long as you are quiet and respectful if you are ever fortunate enough to interact with them. While they will never be tame, the stags especially seem to like a certain amount of human contact, coming quite close from curiosity, though the doe deer are much more shy.

The white hart is a pure white stag which is said to hold magical powers. It is a popular icon of medieval art and literature, and a symbol of the hunt. In some depictions the white hart holds the full moon between his antlers, and as the monarch of the glen, he is said to be a royal beast. Magically speaking, he is of course an aspect of the Horned God of witchcraft. As a power animal he can be invoked for issues of self-worth, pride, protection, courage, abundance and prosperity.

Stags have long been linked to royalty and were often hunted by kings and queens and their royal guests at court. They are even given regal names depending on how well developed their antlers are. The points of the antlers are known as tines and the number of tines determines where the stag is in the hierarchy. A stag with ten tines is known as *a hart of ten*, while less than ten tines indicates a *young buck*. Twelve tines make a *Royal stag*, fourteen tines denote an *Imperial stag*, while sixteen tines crown the majestic *Monarch of the Glen*. The more evenly spaced the tines, the better balanced the stag will be, making him more successful in the rut and therefore more likely to breed. As their antlers are naturally shed each winter, then once the rutting season is over you might find pieces of antler on the forest floor that you can use for altar decorations and craft projects.

Owls

The owl is a bird of two halves. In some cultures, it is said to represent wisdom, magic and alchemical knowledge, while in others it is thought to be a bird of ill omen which brings bad luck. In most places it is considered to be unlucky to see an owl flying during the day. In this respect the owl has a reputation for bringing melancholy on all who see it flying in daylight. As a nocturnal creature the owl is intrinsically linked to the moon, with its round face being reminiscent of the full moon. Some people believe that the owl is an omen of death and there is some truth to this, for it is likely that this association came about because the barn owl in particular will let out a piercing shriek of victory when it has caught its prey. In Scotland the owl is the bird of the Cailleach, the goddess of winter and it is said that she can shapeshift into one of these birds to go around unnoticed. In most cultures owls are associated with goddesses and the Divine Feminine.

Magically, owls are linked to the underworld and the dark half of the year, which is when they are at their most vocal. They are said to be great protectors of magical people, with shamans and druids of the past often wearing an owl feather to denote their standing as a holy man. It is a bird that represents the darker aspects of life; death, winter, night-time, secret knowledge, hidden ways, balance and polarity. As a power animal the owl can be invoked for issues of academic learning, life lessons, dark nights of the soul, shadow craft, inner wisdom, self-awareness, illness, grief and acceptance of a loss.

Frogs and Toads

Frogs and toads are sometimes thought of as ugly creatures and there is a lot of folklore and superstition to suggest that they may have been severely punished for not being attractive enough! In the past it was common to boil a live toad, or impale it on a branch, after rubbing it on to warts. This was thought to remove the wart. Some frogs and toads are toxic and so they were also 'harvested' for their poison too. Frogs tended to fare better than toads, as they were thought to bring good luck, while toads were associated with bad luck. Again, this superstition could simply be down to the fact that frogs have a greater level of *pretty privilege*, which afforded them some protection!

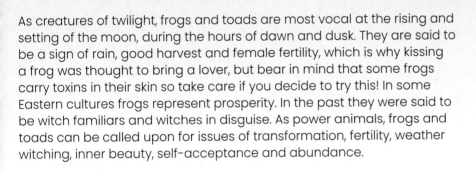

As creatures of twilight, frogs and toads are most vocal at the rising and setting of the moon, during the hours of dawn and dusk. They are said to be a sign of rain, good harvest and female fertility, which is why kissing a frog was thought to bring a lover, but bear in mind that some frogs carry toxins in their skin so take care if you decide to try this! In some Eastern cultures frogs represent prosperity. In the past they were said to be witch familiars and witches in disguise. As power animals, frogs and toads can be called upon for issues of transformation, fertility, weather witching, inner beauty, self-acceptance and abundance.

Hares

Like the wolves who howl at the moon and the cats who hunt in its light, the hare is often mesmerised by lunar light, sitting still and looking up in captivation. To see a moon-gazing hare is said to be extremely fortunate and brings good luck. The hare is a creature of the Divine Feminine and is linked with fertility, spring and regeneration. In medieval times people believed that the image of a hare could be seen on the moon, similarly to the man in the moon.

Traditionally a hare is thought to be an omen of thunderstorms and, in Britain, it is the spirit of the corn, often seen lopping through the stubble after the harvest. Long considered to be witch familiars, it was said that an accused witch would shapeshift into a hare in order to escape her accusers, bounding away before they had a chance to catch her and put her to the rope or the fire. White hares were said to be the spirits of young women who were jilted or betrayed by their lovers. The white hare spirit would haunt the faithless lover in his dreams until he went mad. White hares are also linked with the season of winter, ghosts and death. As a power animal the hare can be called upon for issues of fertility, renewal, magic, divination, escaping a tormentor and going underground or retreating for some quiet time alone.

Moths

Like the butterfly, the moth is a symbol of regeneration, transformation, renewal and rebirth. However, while the butterfly signifies a positive change, the moth indicates transformation through darkness or difficulty. In short the moth represents a dark night of the soul, where someone is changed at a deep level via adversity or illness. This transformation leads to a stronger character and a rebirth of some kind.

Although some moths fly during the day, particularly on dull days during the darker months of the year, they are generally nocturnal creatures. A day flying moth can be distinguished from a butterfly by the way it rests with its wings laid flat and horizontal like a jet, while a butterfly rests with its wings folded vertically. Moths can also be just as colourful as butterflies, but their colours tend to be more muted in tone, to help them blend into the darkness.

They navigate their flight by moonlight, which is why they are naturally drawn to all forms of light. When they circle your lightbulb, they think it is caused by the moon's glow, so they try to reach the deeper darkness on the other side of the light. They will circle the light to the point of exhaustion, so they become their own demise. In some cultures, the moth symbolises death and misfortune. For the most part though, they are simply a winged creature of the night, trying to find their way in the world. As a lunar power animal, they can be called upon for fresh starts, rebirth, transformation and guidance through a dark night of the soul.

Bats

Bats are considered to be creatures associated with the Underworld and, as such, they are linked to the goddess Persephone. They can easily be identified by their erratic flight, which gave rise to their country name of *flitter-mouse*. Often you will see them at dusk, just as night begins to fall, particularly during the summer months when there are lots of insects and moths for them to feed on.

Like wolves and toads, bats have been much maligned in folklore and literature, being linked to vampirism, witchcraft, demons and satanic rites. However, they are beautiful, harmless creatures and to watch them flittering across the sky at dusk is a sight well worth seeing. They tend to get dehydrated quite quickly, so if you find one on the ground, offer it some water in a shallow bowl or using a pipette. Wear gloves when you do this as they do tend to bite – that part isn't a myth! You can also offer a little dog or cat food to help revive the bat. I have hand-fed bats myself when I worked in a veterinary clinic, and it is such a privilege to help them in this way, and to see the tiny mouth gaping open for more water. They are incredibly sweet! They recover quite quickly and will soon be fit to fly again, once rehydrated.

Bats tend to live in colonies, so where you see one, others won't be that far behind. They prefer to live in tall trees and old buildings such as churches, castle ruins and derelict property. All bats and their roosts are legally protected throughout the UK and Europe, which means that you cannot clear or harm a colony, but must leave them undisturbed. As power animals, they can be called upon for navigation and finding your own path, intuition, networking and facing fears. There are lots of bat-spotting events held during the summer months, so if this interests you go along and see how many bats you can identify. Alternatively, sit in a garden or meadow as dusk falls and wait for them to appear in the night sky.

Swans

Although swans are more active during the day, they also like to move around at dusk and dawn, which is when they tend to journey between one body of water and another in search of food. If you have ever seen a swan gliding silently across a loch or lake under a full moon, you will be aware of what a ghostly and ethereal presence they can have. Often, this nocturnal gliding is the job of a male swan, patrolling the area around his mate and their nest, especially if they have cygnets to protect.

In Scottish folklore, swans are said to be the reincarnated spirits of women who died in childbirth. They are associated with the Celtic god Aenghus and his beloved wife, Caer, a fairy-maid, who could both turn into swans and are deities of true love. Swans are associated with purity, fidelity, loyalty, love, strength, honour, the spirit realms and the moon, so they can be called upon for help with all these things. In the UK, Mute swans come under the protection of the reigning monarch and all swans are a protected species in general.

These are just a few of the animals that are associated with the moon. There are many more so feel free to do your own research. Working with power animals can be an extremely rewarding practice, as you begin to learn more about your chosen creature and its unique strategies for survival. It is a valuable aspect of a natural magical practice, and as your animal communicates with you through dreams and visions, don't be surprised if your dreams become more vivid after calling on them in this way.

PART

16

MOON RITUALS

Beautiful and mesmeric, powerful and magnetic, the moon deserves to be celebrated in ritual. In witchcraft we call rituals that honour the moon Esbats. Each month witches will work rituals to welcome and honour certain lunar phases, predominantly the new and full moon. We also like to make the most of special moons, such as blue moons and super moons. Dark moon is considered to be a time of rest, but even this is a way to honour her because the dark moon represents the fallow period before a new season of growth. In resting during the dark moon, witches are honouring that phase by their lack of action. In this chapter we will look at some of the most common forms of Esbat ritual.

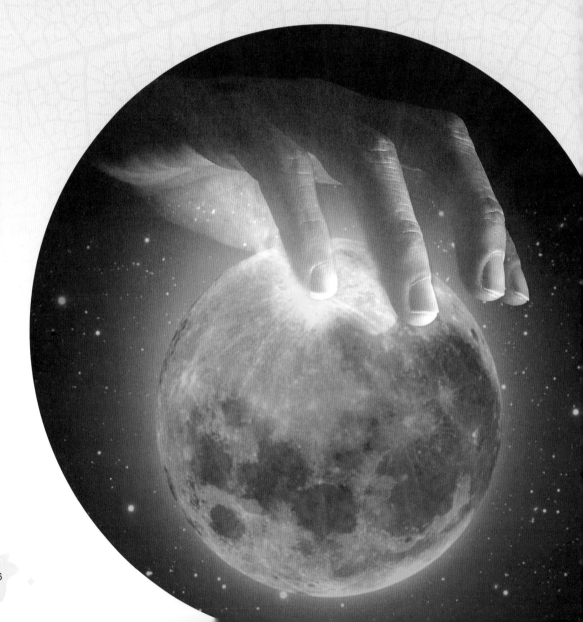

Drawing Down the Moon

Drawing down the moon is a full moon Esbat and it is a key aspect of Wiccan practice. It is a form of spiritual channelling, wherein the practitioner invokes the lunar goddess energies into themselves for greater power. This power is then redirected into spellcraft. This Esbat is about welcoming the power of the full moon into yourself and your life. It could be described as a more active form of moon bathing, where you take the moon's energy into yourself, rather than just basking in her silvery rays. When done correctly a sense of deep calm is experienced, along with a strong pull toward your destiny. This is why people sometimes change their mind about the type of spell they're going to cast after drawing down the moon, because the lunar energies are guiding them towards a higher path. If this happens to you, just go with it and trust that you are being guided to cast the kind of spell that is for your highest good, one that will have the best outcome for you in the long term.

To draw down the moon you will need to have a clear view of the full moon, so you should ideally work this ritual outdoors. Traditionally you would use an athame, which is a witch's ritual blade, but you can also use your hand. Stand and gaze at the moon until you feel relaxed and centred. Then hold your arms out to the moon, pointing your athame or holding your hands out towards it as if you are going to capture the light. Visualize the moon's energies surging down the blade or through your hands into your body. Take mental note of any particular feelings you experience, such as tingling excitement or a calm sense of purpose. Once you feel that you are full of lunar energies, give thanks and lower your arms. Welcome the full moon with the following words:

I welcome the goddess of full lunar light

I cast in your name this sacred night

You are now ready to cast your chosen spells, using the lunar energies within you as a power boost to your magic. Traditionally women would draw down the moon, while men would draw down the sun during a midday ritual. However, in recent years, it has become more common for either sex to draw down the energies of either the moon or the sun.

New Moon Esbat Ritual

New moon Esbats tend to be all about intentionality. At this time, you should decide what it is that you want the lunar energies to bring your way through the course of the coming month. Asking the moon to guide you to your goals is a great way to begin any spell work for goals, ambitions and manifestation.

On the night of the new moon, write down your intentions for the month and what you hope to accomplish. Once you have your goals written down, roll the paper into a scroll, light the end and allow it to burn in a heatproof dish or cauldron, as you say:

New moon of lunar light

Bring me a month of success so bright

Scatter the ashes to the sky and know that you have set your intentions and you have the magic of the moon on your side.

Blue Moon Esbat

The blue moon is the magical moon of manifestation! When there are two full moons in any one calendar month, the second is called the blue moon. It usually only occurs every couple of years, hence the saying *once in a blue moon*. Because it is rare, it is considered to be a most auspicious time for goal-setting, spell-casting and general manifestation. To tap into the sacred power of this moon witches usually cast spells for big ambitions and long term goals. This is the time to cast for a new house, a change in location, a marriage, a career change and so on. Basically, if it feels too big for you to achieve on your own and you have no idea how you can bring your dream into reality, then you need to harness the power of a blue moon.

For this ritual you will need an egg and a marker pen. On the night of the blue moon, write your big ambition on the shell of the egg. Reduce the ambition down to one or two key words or a brief sentence if possible, so you might write *I work from home*, or *I am a mother*. Be sure to write your goal in the present tense as if it has already happened. Next, take the egg outside into the garden or an earthy space, dig a small hole and bury the egg in the earth saying:

As the blue moon shines in space and time

It lights the way to this dream of mine

As the egg decomposes, it will slowly release the magic that you have cast and the power of the blue moon will begin to shift things around in your favour. This is a great ritual to cast when you know exactly where you want to be in life, but you don't know how to get there. Allow the blue moon energies to smooth out the path for you, so that your goal manifests naturally.

Black Moon Esbat

The Black Moon occurs when two new moons fall within the same calendar month and again this is indicative of a time of rare moments. When the black moon shines you are being given another shot at something that means a lot to you – a second bite of the cherry, so to speak. The Black Moon is the time of second chances, double takes, lucky breaks or the return of an opportunity you thought was lost to you. Keep your eyes peeled for signs that second chances are being offered and help them along with this ritual. Take a pinch of blessing seeds, also known as nigella seeds, outside under the light of the black moon. Think of something in your life that you feel you missed out on, something you regret losing. It could be an old flame, a lost career opportunity or an event you missed. Whatever it is, hold this image in your mind as you look up to the sky and the first sliver of moonlight. Now blow the seeds in the direction of the moon and say:

As a black moon edges into view

A second chance returns anew

Learn from your past mistakes. If fear held you back before, accept the second chance with courage. If you let other things hold you back, step forward into this new opportunity with confidence. Take that second bite of the cherry and enjoy it!

Super Moon Esbat

The Super Moon is linked to achievement and success, so this Esbat is all about manifesting the rewards of your endeavours. However, you will be expected to work hard for your achievements and nothing is going to be handed to you on a plate. This success could come in any area of your life – love, career, business, family life, adventure etc. – but when you welcome the energies of the super moon into your life, know that you are about to experience the kind of power surge that only comes from victory. While feeling victorious is a good thing, it can also make people complacent and arrogant. Take care not to let this level of success go to your head and keep your ego in check. To welcome the super moon, burn three dried bay leaves on a charcoal block and say:

I welcome the surge of a super moon

Hear my request and grant this boon

(state your goal)

Bay leaves are symbolic of victory, so burning them in offering will ensure that you are victorious in your own endeavours and ambitions. This powerful moon can guide you towards your destiny, so pay attention to the dreams you have during this moon as they may hold key messages from the Divine Feminine.

Planetary Influences

Alongside the moon, the planets can also have an influence on you and how you view the world. Each planet represents a different aspect of character and you can draw on certain planetary energies to give you a boost in that area. For instance, if you were looking for love, you would work with Venus, lighting candles and incense as offerings to this planetary goddess and invoking her in your rituals. Here are the main planets and how they can be used to build up your character, helping you to become a well-rounded individual who isn't easily fazed by life's little stumbles.

◇ Sun – rules your self-image and confidence
◇ Moon – rules your emotional intelligence
◇ Mercury – rules your intellect and how you communicate with others
◇ Venus – rules your ability to give and receive love and open up to others
◇ Mars – rules your world view and assertiveness
◇ Jupiter – rules your destiny and luck
◇ Saturn – rules your self-discipline and sense of personal responsibility
◇ Uranus – rules your individuality and self-expression
◇ Neptune – rules your imagination and dreams
◇ Pluto – rules your self-actualization, motivation and ambition

Little Star

Wishing on stars is something lots of people have done without even being aware that they are casting a spell! It is something that we teach children to do from a very young age and many cultures throughout history, including the Greeks and Egyptians, believed in its power. So what have you got to lose? Here are some ways that you can start wishing on stars.

◇ Wish on the first star you see each night. This is usually the planet Venus, who shines brightest at dusk and dawn. Gaze at her beauty and make that wish.

◇ Wish on the constellation of your astrological sign. These are thestars that you were born under so you are naturally attuned to their energies.

◇ Wish on a shooting star. These are actually meteor showers which shoot across the night sky. Meteor shower calendars are available online, so you can look up when the next one is due, to give yourself the best chance of seeing these stunning 'shooting stars'.

The Moon as a Muse

For some people, the moon is an essential collaborator in their creative pursuits. There is something almost sacred about working on a creative project after dark, when the moon rides high in the sky and all the world below is quiet and still. The peace that comes as night falls is vital for writers, artists, musicians, poets, witches and so on. Many people find comfort in their hobbies in the evenings, picking up needlework projects, art therapy or spell-craft when the working day is over. Indeed, the hours of darkness might be the only free time they have to indulge in a creative activity.

Artistic magic happens best by moon light, when the silvery shadows call to mind enchanted portals and ghostly apparitions that feed the imagination and inspire creativity. Many pieces of music, my own *Winter's Nocturne* included, often have nocturnal words in their title, indicating that they were composed to represent the beauty of the night. Beethoven's *Moonlight Sonata* is one example, while the numerous *Nocturnes* of Chopin are another.

The same is true for some artwork. Consider well known paintings such as *Night with Her Train of Stars* or *Night* both by Edward Hughes, or perhaps Vincent van Gogh's *The Starry Night*, or Claude Monet's *Seascape: Shipping by Moonlight* for instance. With all their moody black and blue tones, it's easy to see the inspirational effect the moon has had on artists down the centuries.

Working throughout the night is a natural process for many creative people, especially those who make a living from their art. Sometimes the daytime is just too bright and busy to get much work done, and so the darkness colludes with us to make artistry and creativity easier. In this way, the moon becomes a muse to the artist or writer, shining down her light of inspiration.

You can tap into this energy, weaving the moon-glow into your own creative projects by working at night-time. Create a nice routine, where you gather together any materials you need for your project, or go into your creative workspace if you have one, then create a cosy atmosphere in which to work. Grab a hot drink, maybe a blanket to snuggle into as you work, light scented candles or incense and a softly glowing lamp, then set your creativity to work. Repeat this routine every night over the course of a few weeks or months and you will be surprised by how quickly your project progresses. To help you along, cast the following spell to invoke the lunar light into your creative hobby or occupation.

Invoke Lunar Light for Creativity

Make your creative space all ready for your work and if possible, allow the moonlight to come into the room, or at least leave the blinds open to the night sky. Next, light a tea-light and place it in a holder. Set this within your working area and say these words, or something similar. Repeat the invocation every time you work on your project in the evenings.

By lunar light and moon-glow bright

I call the muse of silver light

Creative magic now sealed in starlight

I invoke the muse of the moon this night.

Astral Projection

Astral projection, also known as astral travel or an out of body experience, is the idea that the astral body, or consciousness, can leave the physical body for a short time, giving rise to the dream-like sensation of floating or flying. Some people experience this during times of Rapid Eye Movement (REM) sleep. Spontaneous out of body experiences seem to be more likely during times of high stress or illness. It can also be experienced when a person is under anaesthetic during an operation, allowing the sleeping patient to look down on the scene and watch from above.

Although astral projection and out of body experiences seem to occur quite naturally as we sleep, some people believe that it can be induced deliberately, or ritualistically, allowing them to go on nocturnal rambles and meet up with other astral travellers along the way. While there is currently no scientific evidence that astral projection actually exists, lots of people claim to have had these type of out of body experiences. It is thought that this is where common dreams of flying, falling, floating and levitating originate from.

In certain indigenous cultures, astral travel is actively encouraged and may even be induced with the use of special herbal concoctions. The Native Americans referred to this kind of psychic journey as a vision quest, or dream-walking and it was seen as a valuable tool of insight and self-discovery.

Astral travellers are said to be able to connect more easily with other ethereal beings, such as angels, spirit guides, ghosts, faeries, even aliens. This is because the ethereal self has fewer inhibitions and fears, so it is more open to such experiences. In spirit form, the astral traveller is also thought to have the ability to see glimpses of the past and the future, during psychic visions that are clearly remembered upon waking.

It is commonly believed that the astral self is tethered to the physical body by a silver cord, similar to the umbilical cord. This silver cord ensures that the astral self doesn't stray too far from its physical host. Furthermore, should the physical body be in any danger or detect any sign of threat, then the silver cord instantly pulls the astral-self back into the body, meaning that the sleeper experiences a swooping sensation and wakes with a startled jump. This can be quite unnerving, but it is actually a natural reaction known as a hypnic jerk or a sleep start. Here are a few things to bear in mind if you want to try more intentional astral projection.

Tips for Astral Projection

◇ Make sure that you are calm and relaxed. Don't try this technique when you are stressed or poorly.

◇ Sip a cup of valerian tea about half an hour before trying to astral project.

◇ Lay down in a comfortable position.

◇ Spray your pillow with an infusion of lemongrass and vervain essential oils mixed in water, as these herbs are said to aid psychic visions and astral travel.

◇ Ensure the room is at a good temperature, so not too hot or too cold.

◇ Call on your angels and spirit guides to watch over you and protect you.

◇ Put a little Moon Dust powder (see page 218) into a pouch and keep this with you for protection, as you nod off to sleep.

◇ Think of a place or person you would like to visit as your astral self.

◇ Arrange to 'meet' a friend on the astral plane one night.

◇ Hold that image in your mind as you begin to fall asleep.

◇ Tell yourself that you are going on an astral journey to this place or person.

◇ Tell yourself that you will remember your astral adventures when you wake up.

◇ Allow yourself to gently drift off to sleep. Happy travelling!

Moon Dust for Protection

Moon dust is a popular spell powder, commonly made up of egg shells, salt, ash and sometimes glitter. Eggs shells are frequently used in protection spells because they are designed to protect new life. For this spell you will need a few dried, cleaned out eggs shells – be sure to remove the entire membrane and allow the egg shells to dry thoroughly. When ready, grind the shells up using a mortar and pestle. Add a teaspoon of sea salt, ashes from your favourite incense and mix it all together. If you wish, you can add a little glitter too but, if doing so, remember that the values of natural magic means you should use biodegradeable glitter rather than the older, polluting variety.

Once mixed up, decant the moon dust powder into a clean, airtight jar and label it accordingly. To charge the powder with lunar energy, set the jar in the light of the moon, from one full moon to the next full moon. You can then use it as a protection powder by scattering it around outside your home, in your car, in a loved one's shoes or by rolling candles in it for a protection spell.

Moon dust is also very good for wishing spells. Simply take a pinch of it in the palm of your hand, go outside in the evening and make a wish to the night sky as you blow the moon dust away to carry your wish out to the stars.

MOON DUST FCR PROTECTION

PART
17

MOON
FABLES

Fables, legends and folklore are full of enchantment and magic. Often the moon plays a significant role within these stories. Not only are fables the bedrock of storytelling and literature, they are also useful teaching tools, passing down nuggets of wisdom and wise advice to the younger generation. Fables especially tend to hold a kernel of truth or wisdom within the body of the text. In *The Boy Who Cried Wolf* for instance, the message is clear: don't cry for attention needlessly, otherwise when you actually need help no-one will come to your assistance. In *The Fox and the Wolf*, the cunning fox persuades his cousin the wolf that the reflection of the moon in the lake is actually a large round of cheese. Eager to get to the cheese, the wolf drinks the entire lake and promptly bursts. The twin message of this fable is don't be greedy and don't believe everything you're told!

The most famous fables are of course, *Aesop's Fables*, which were written by a storyteller in ancient Greece. As a result, Aesop is credited with being the originator of this type of moral tale. His fables usually feature anthropomorphic animals and fantastical creatures from mythology and legend. Rudyard Kipling's *Just So Stories* were published much later, in 1902, yet they follow a similar pattern, using fables to explain various animal behaviours, anatomies and characteristics.

Some fables also include ghostly visitations, supernatural creatures and spirits from another world. These tales were especially popular from medieval times up to the early 20th century and would be told around the fireplace on cold winter nights. In these more phantasmagorical stories, the original innocent animals from earlier fables became demonic messengers from hell. Such tales were used by the Church as dire warnings of what would happen if someone strayed outside the fold of Christianity. This type of storytelling was designed to keep people faithful to the Church. It was also used as propaganda during the witch hunts when beloved pets were regarded as witch's familiars and therefore, proof of witchcraft. Thus began the demonization of beautiful creatures such as wolves, cats, bats, snakes and rats.

The Fabled Moon

The moon is often a key feature in many fables and folklore, with fairies, werewolves, vampires, witches and ghosts all said to be more active during the magical phase of the full moon. Certain superstitions came about as a result of these legends. For instance, one superstition states that you should never step inside a circle of toadstools on the night of the full moon or the faeries will steal you away. Another claims that if you wander through the woods during the time of the Hunter's Moon in autumn, the ghostly Wild Hunt might mistake you for a wayward spirit and carry you back to the Underworld, kicking and screaming. And we all know what happens if you get bitten by a wolf on the night of the full moon! In this chapter then, we are going to explore some of these fabled tales and superstitions.

Lycanthropy

There are many tales of lycanthropy in folklore, which is the legend of people turning into werewolves during the time of the full moon. This transformation usually occurs only after the individual has been bitten by a wolf, though there are also tales of lycanthropy being an inherited condition, passed down from one generation to the next.

In Europe during the Middle Ages, belief in werewolves was so strong that trials for lycanthropy were not uncommon. While women were targeted by the witch hunters and tried for witchcraft, men were sometimes charged with the crime of lycanthropy. In both instances, the accused were usually impoverished individuals with no-one to speak up for them. In lycanthropy trials torture was often used as a means of gaining a confession and the punishment on conviction included being flayed alive and then beheaded. The head would be set upon a spike as a warning to others, while the rest of the body would then be burned at the stake in a public display of victory to demonstrate the collective power of the authorities, and the Church, over the individual.

Just as with the witch trials, lycanthropy trials were a form of social cleansing and a good way to dispatch any troublesome old tramp, hermit or suspected criminal. During this period of history, the term *wolfshead* was used to denote a criminal, though the crime could be something as innocuous as hunting the king's deer or poaching a rabbit.

In the past, fear of wolves wasn't entirely unfounded because when large packs of wolves roamed the countryside during a harsh winter, they would sometimes feed on untended livestock, pets, possibly even small children, all of which provided the wolves with an easy meal. This added fuel to the fire of superstition and the belief in werewolves, along with their subsequent lycanthropy trials, only began to diminish once the wolves themselves were hunted almost to the point of extinction.

Thankfully the wolf has survived and they are now a protected species, happily roaming free in the mountainous regions of Russia, Eastern Europe, parts of America and the French Alps. A protected pack of wolves can also be found in a conservation wildlife sanctuary in Shropshire in the UK.

Far from being supernatural, in the modern world lycanthropy is now viewed as a psychiatric mental health condition, in which the patient has delusions of being able to turn into a wolf or some other kind of large predator, usually canine, though not always. During these psychotic episodes the patient may exhibit animalistic behaviours such as crawling on all fours, howling and snarling. This mental health condition is extremely rare and it is usually treated with psychiatric medication. That said, the superstition that a full moon can make people crazy and lead to erratic and questionable behaviour is still in circulation today, but there is no scientific evidence as yet to prove this theory.

The Wild Hunt

Probably one of the spookiest aspects of folklore, The Wild Hunt is well known in various mythologies, including Scottish, Irish, Welsh, Germanic and Norse. As the name suggests, the Wild Hunt is a hunting party, but one that you would not want to saddle up for! It is a spectral Hunt, led by a phantom Horseman, with a pack of ghostly hounds running alongside his midnight black mount. Legend states that both horse and hounds have glowing red eyes and foaming mouths, while the Horseman is hooded – or headless!

To see or hear the Wild Hunt has long been considered to be a bad omen and although it can be encountered at any time of year, it is more usual for this legend to resurface during the dark autumn and winter months, especially during the time of the Hunter's Moon in October. The Wild Hunt rides in on the billowing clouds of a storm-filled sky. The eerie sound of the hunting horn blows in on the wind, trumpeting through the treetops. The Wild Hunt's purpose is to gather up the souls of the dead and carry them away to the Otherworld.

The Horseman who leads the Hunt is by turns Arawn, Cernunnos, Herne the Hunter, Gwyn ap Nudd, Odin or Woden depending on the region and culture. In Ireland he is associated with Dullachan, a headless horseman who wanders the byways looking for lost souls to take. Again, the Dullachan, or Dark Man, was said to be a harbinger of death. This links back to the *dark man dreams* or nightmares of shadowy figures that we looked at earlier, being linked with anxiety, worry, depression, despair and melancholia, so heed this message from your subconscious if you experience such dreams on a regular basis, and seek out help if you need it.

It is safe to say that Washington Irving was probably inspired by the folklore of the Wild Hunt when he wrote *The Legend of Sleepy Hallow* and the Hunt remains a prevalent aspect of spooky folklore. While you are unlikely to see the Hunt in full force, you might experience hints of it – in the shapes of storm clouds or the sound of the autumn wind blowing through the forests and hills. It was said that hiding in a kirk or church would protect one from the Hunt as it rode by, but avoid sheltering under yew trees, for they are portals through which the Huntsman rides and you will put yourself directly in his path!

Faerie Revels

The faeries are also said to be more active during the time of the full moon and this is when the Faerie Host is supposed to ride out in the evening. Also known as the Faerie Troop, and similar to the Wild Hunt, these trooping faeries ride their fey horses, unicorns and kelpies about the countryside, traversing from one faerie mound or hill to another. Should you get in their way, they will carry you off into Elphame or faerie-land, as their prisoner. The Scottish *Tale of Tam Lin* is perhaps the most well-known fable that recounts this type of abduction.

Signs that the Faerie Host is near include hearing the sound of faerie bells and the jingling of harness, with no obvious source for the sound. In addition, hearing the blast of a hunting horn is said to herald the arrival of the Faerie Troop, who are the knights of Elphame. In Celtic folklore these faeries are spilt into two courts, the benevolent Seelie Court and the malevolent Unseelie Court. Crossing paths with either Court on a full moon night was best avoided.

There are also thought to be other fey beings such as sprites, pixies, nixies, elves and brownies out and about during a full moon. These faeries can be helpful towards humans and often grant wishes or help with chores. However, they can be tricksters too, enjoying nothing better than playing pranks on unsuspecting humans. These types of faeries like to gather in faerie rings, which are circles of toadstools, or sometimes stone circles, where they dance, feast and hold faerie revels. Often they will invite humans to join their party, but if you dance with the fey or eat their food, legend says that you will waste away, longing only for faerie food and frolic, while the human world becomes dull and unsatisfying. Christina Rossetti's poem *Goblin Market* was inspired by this aspect of British folklore and states that:

We must not look at goblin men,

We must not buy their fruits:

Who knows upon what soil they fed

Their hungry, thirsty roots?

All in all, it is probably better *not* to step into a faerie ring if you should ever come across one, especially if the moon is full!

White Ladies

Tales of ghostly ladies dressed in flowing, diaphanous white gowns are a common aspect of folklore, told throughout the world. Known as *White Ladies* or *The Woman in White*, they are frequently associated with historical figures who died in tragic circumstances and are left haunting the area where they once lived.

These ghostly Women in White are said to appear on nights when the moon is bright or haloed by mist. They have been linked to pagan sabbats such as Litha on the summer solstice, Mabon on the autumnal equinox and Samhain on October 31st. Such pagan apparitions could be linked with the Maiden aspect of the Triple Goddess.

In some legends they are the spirits of women who died in childbirth, or at the hands of violent men, while in others, they are the ghosts of women who committed suicide or whose death was caused by drowning. The latter is more common when the White Lady haunts an area close to a body of water. In more modern renditions of this legend, the White Lady is said to have been a victim of a road traffic accident and she appears to hitchhike or catch a lift from a passing vehicle, only to suddenly disappear again moments later.

Traditionally associated with ancient castles, abbeys and old stately homes, White Ladies tend to wander through the grounds and along roadsides, presumably scaring the local people with their sudden spectral appearance! In some legends she is said to be a harbinger of death or doom, similar to the Celtic Ban Sidhe or banshee. Occasionally she is associated with some kind of curse connected to a particular clan or noble family.

White Ladies are also linked to the Reformation and King Henry VIII's dissolution of the monasteries and abbeys, where they are thought to be nuns who died protecting their home during the violent destruction of the abbey. In some instances, the White Lady is thought to be guarding some kind of treasure or hidden wealth, which ties in with the theme of nuns trying to guard the wealth of their abbey and the Catholic Church.

Whatever her origin may be, the Woman in White has been seen all over the world, yet her preference for appearing to unwary travellers seems to be on dark nights in isolated areas and beneath the silvery glow of the moon, which lends an ethereal charm to her ghostly apparel. So if you happen to be driving along a country road at night, be wary of offering someone a lift!

Ghost Soldiers

Another spectre that has links to the moon is that of the ghost soldier. It should come as no surprise that old battlefields, such as Culloden Moor and Bannockburn in Scotland, or Gettysburg in the United States, might still carry an eerie atmosphere, given the sheer number of men who lost their lives in those locations. However, the dead don't always lie peacefully and there have been sightings of ghostly soldiers still doing battle, centuries after the wars were lost and won. In Gibraltar there is talk of the ghost of a British Army Officer walking his dog through the tunnels that were dug to protect people during air raids in the Second World War. He is said to be an omen of good luck and protection.

Some ghost soldiers date back even further, to the time of the Roman invasion of Britain, with troops of Roman soldiers said to haunt the M6 motorway. It is also thought that the Roman Ninth Legion, which mysteriously disappeared without trace, haunts the area around Hadrian's Wall in the UK, forever marching north to Scotland.

In more recent times the legend has developed and now the phantom soldier seems to have taken on a new task – that of guiding serving soldiers through dangerous terrain and enemy territory where improvised explosive devices (IEDs) are buried underground. This phantom appears out of nowhere wearing a uniform the soldiers recognise and understand to be an ally, then he leads the soldiers to safety, before disappearing.

The 1986 song *Camouflage* by Stan Ridgeway is a fictional account of this kind of ghost soldier.

It's not just soldiers' spirits that seem to linger either. In Oxfordshire, an old aircraft hangar that was formerly a part of RAF Grove, is said to be haunted by the ghost of an American airman from the Second World War, while a pilot from the First World War is thought to haunt the air station in Montrose, Scotland.

It's no secret that the military take the moon phase into consideration when planning their missions and they use it to their advantage whenever they can. During the Second World War, before the development of GPS, RAF pilots would use the full moon to aid navigation during their night flights. It makes sense then that ghostly soldiers and servicemen should appear under a full moon in places where battles have taken place, because for the military the full moon is often a time of activity and great risk. While guidance from a spooky phantom saviour might not be exactly *welcome*, I'm sure the warning is appreciated nonetheless!

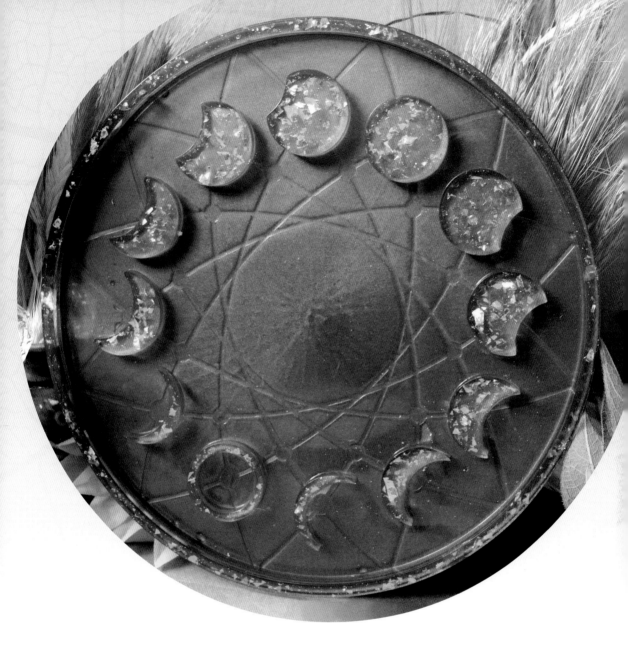

PART
18

MOON
MEDITATIONS

Lunar light is a well-known conduit for visions and intuitive dreams among psychics and seers. Many people find that they experience more vivid dreams around the time of the waxing to full moon, particularly if the moonlight shines into their bedroom. This lunar enhancement of psychic visions can be used during meditation. Guided meditations are great for strengthening your ability to visualize and they are good for gaining insight. Often the higher self will throw up symbols and messages while you are meditating too, which you can interpret after the meditation.

I have designed the guided meditations in this chapter to be gentle and ethereal paths to personal insight and enlightenment. These are mental journeys to magical, imaginary realms. They can be linked together or used interchangeably. Each meditation has its own kind of insight to offer, but this will come from your own intuition, so you need to be open-minded. You can either record them and playback the recording when you want to use the meditation, or you can work with a like-minded partner and have them read it out loud as you meditate. Then you do the same for them. The meditations are linked to particular issues.

◇ For ambition and goals use Once Upon a Winter's Moon
◇ For courage in adversity use Monarch of the Luna Glen
◇ For inspiration and destiny use Midnight Hare
◇ For questions about relationships use Sparkling Swan
◇ For finding your soulmate use Lover's Moon
◇ For direction in a crisis use Soldier's Moon

In the following meditations, you will find gods and goddesses, whimsical animals and fey beings, all of which are linked to the moon. I hope that you enjoy working with these extra-special lunar journeys of enchantment.

Once Upon a Winter's Moon

You find yourself standing upon a sandy beach as darkness falls. The full moon is high over the water as the waves crash in to shore. It is a cold night and winter is just beginning. Your breath mists the air as you begin to walk along the rocky coastline, the grey rocks looming high in the moonlight between land and sea. The sound of the ocean is soothing to you and you enjoy its endless melody as the waves roll in and then recede.

As you walk, you notice a new light on the horizon. At first it is just a glimmer in the blackness of the sky, but soon it grows brighter. It is unlike any light you have ever seen before, glimmering and shimmering over the ocean. As the light develops in shades of blue and green and gold, you realize that you are witnessing the Northern Lights and you stop to admire them. The light swirls around the skyline, going this way and that, with sudden changes in direction as it turns back upon itself. It reminds you of the starling murmurations in autumn, but this movement comes from the ethereal lights in the sky, rather than from a flock of birds. It is mesmerizing and enchanting. The light reflects upon the water, but you cannot tear your eyes away from the Firefox of the night sky, as it dances around the heavens.

Suddenly you hear the gentle hooting of an owl behind you and turning, you see a ghostly shape flying towards you. It is a pure white owl. It lands on one of the rocks and hoots again, almost as if it is greeting you. It has eyes of icy Arctic blue and around its neck is a silver snowflake charm. This is no ordinary owl and you nod your head in respect and say "Merry Meet, Wise One." The owl hoots again, then swiftly takes to the sky once more, swooping down to the beach and perching on another rock, closer to the sea. You follow the bird and say, "As beautiful as you are, Wise One, I know that you are more than you seem. Will you not show yourself to me, that I may get to know you better?" The owl launches itself into the air, where it swiftly transforms into a beautiful woman. She is tall and slender, dressed in a gown of silver and white. Her hair is such a pale shade of blonde, it is almost silver, yet she does not look old. She appears ageless, her icy blue eyes are full of wisdom and knowledge.

"Merry Meet, Seeker of the Old Ones. I am Arianrhod, lady of the Silver Wheel and the Stars. I am the one who turns the Wheel of the Year. I weave the tapestry of all life at my sacred silver loom. I turn the tides of the oceans and the tides of your life. I send you the wondrous gifts that change your future – the golden opportunities, the dreams come true and the wishes made manifest, all come from my light."

You thank the goddess for her gifts and thinking back over your life thus far, you tell her which special gifts, talents and opportunities have meant the most to you and why. You tell her what you have done with her gifts and how you have used them to improve your life, and the lives of others. Express your gratitude for all that you have and all that she has given to you over the years.

"You're most welcome, Seeker, for it gives me great pleasure to help you achieve all your dreams. Dreaming is what winter nights were made for! I see all your dreams, I know where your ambitions lie and if you trust me and follow my light, I will guide you to achieve everything that is for your highest good. See those lights on the horizon, the ones that swirl in green and gold, the ones that humans call Firefox and Mirrie Dancers? Those are my lights and they are the portal to my realm. Would you like to see them more closely?"

Arianrhod's icy blue eyes are twinkling in the moonlight as she holds her hand out to you. You nod, take her hand and she leads you further down the beach to the water's edge.

"Will you help me to summon my steeds, Seeker? They aren't far away, but sometimes they can be a little wild and unruly. Will you help me to call them and bring them forth?"

"Yes, I will." Hand in hand with Arianrhod, you both raise your arms high above your heads in invocation, facing out to sea. In a soft voice that sounds like the whispering of gentle waves, Arianrhod begins to chant and you join in with her, saying the words:

Come Starlight, come Moonlight, come Luna and Glisten

Heed the sea's call, come forth as you listen

White horses fly forward on wave upon wave

Mane-tossed and charging, hearts beating brave

Come forth as the strength of the wild ocean's might

Come forth and fly high on this cold winter's night.

As soon as the chant is finished, you notice that the sea begins to surge and bubble, like soup in a cauldron. The waves swell and plunge, then the white cresting foam takes on the shape of four wild, white horses, silver hooves beating upon the surface of the water as they charge out of the sea, tossing their manes and flicking their tails. Behind them is a snow white carriage, shaped like a crescent moon, hung with silver star lanterns on either side that cast an ethereal glow.

You gaze in wonder at such magic! The four white horses stand in their silver traces, tossing their heads and snorting, eager to be off on an adventure. Arianrhod soothes each one with a whisper and a caress or a pat. Then she turns to you and says "Come, Seeker of the Old Ones. Ride with me and see the magic of my realm." Eagerly, you climb into the Crescent Moon carriage and settle back in your seat. Arianrhod tucks a blanket of white fur around you both, takes up the reins and with a click of her tongue, the horses move off into a swift gallop, pulling the carriage behind them. They gallop along the length of the beach and then, with a mighty leap, they are up in the air and galloping across the sky.

You hang over the side of the lunar carriage and look down in wonder as the sandy beach disappears below you and the rocks become specks of darkness, as the horses ascend higher and higher. It is the most exhilarating feeling you have ever experienced. Arianrhod guides the horses straight towards the Northern Lights on the horizon and, in mere moments, you are in the thick of them, surrounded by glimmering green and gold as you travel down a long tunnel of vibrant Northern light. At the end of the tunnel stands a many-turreted castle, its spires reaching for the stars that surround it. Made from crystal and ice, it shimmers and gleams like a glacier against the backdrop of the midnight black sky.

Arianrhod pulls up the horses and the carriage stops at the foot of the steps that lead to the castle door. "Welcome to Caer Sidi, the castle of starlight. Come, let me show you around." You leap from the carriage and give a quick pat to the horses, before following Arianrhod and ascending the steps to the castle entrance. The door swings open of its own accord. "It knows me." Arianrhod explains, "Its magic is attuned with mine, just as the magic of your home is attuned with you."

Wandering through the door, you find yourself in a towering great hall. There is a blue-flamed fire burning at one end and in the middle is a table, with two goblets set on a silver tray. Arianrhod picks up the goblets and hands one to you. It is filled with a green liquid that seems to smoke in a vapour that smells vaguely of aniseed and vanilla. "Metheglin, the faerie drink," says Arianrhod. "It is a potion to help visions and inspiration. Drink, Seeker, for who knows what visions of the future might be waiting for you, just beyond the tipple!"

You sip the metheglin and enjoy the warmth it gives to you, then ask, "What is the purpose of this place, this castle of starlight? What happens here?"

"This is a place of rest, Seeker. Rest for the fallen until they are ready to be reborn into a new life. Rest for the weary until they are able to lift up their spirits once more. It is here in my castle where dreams rest and wait, until the person they are meant for is ready to receive them. Would you like to see my Library of Dreams?"

"Are my dreams kept there?"

"All dreams are kept there safely, watching and waiting, until they are needed. Come, let me show you." She sets down her goblet and walks across the great hall, with you following close behind. There, hidden behind a great tapestry, is a large silver door, carved with magical runes and sigils. Arianrhod opens the door and steps aside, allowing you to enter the room first.

You find yourself in the biggest library you have ever seen. Shelves stretch up higher than the eye can see and each one is filled with scrolls, rather than books. The shelves are sectioned off by subject, but these are not the subjects found in most libraries. Instead you see that sections are labelled in the following way. Dreams; Goals; Ambitions; Talents; Academics; Careers; Wishes; Opportunities; Serendipity; Familiars; Soul Mates; and so on. You wander around the shelves, wondering where your own dreams are kept. As if she can read your thoughts, Arianrhod says "They are **all** yours, Seeker. Anything you choose to be and do and achieve, begins right here in this room. This is where your wondrous dreams come true. Look around, find your heart's desire... everything is available to you now, but choose wisely."

You make your way to the section of the library that best fits your own personal dreams and ambition. Arianrhod follows you and says, "Ah yes, I thought you might be drawn here. Choose a destiny-scroll to take with you, Seeker, as my gift to you." You pick out a scroll and tuck it into your belt, thanking the goddess as you do so, for this scroll is the assurance that your dream will soon come true.

"And now we must part ways, Seeker of the Old Ones. Look for me in the Northern Star, make a wish and know that Caer Sidi and I will always be here to help you to make your dreams a reality. Come, and I will show you the way back to your own realm."

You follow Arianrhod out onto a balcony, where there is a slide made from starlight. You recognize it as the Milky Way. You turn to thank Arianrhod one last time and she pulls you into a warm hug and says; "Sit for a spell in the starlight, Seeker, and think of me when you do. Now let the Milky Way carry you safe to your own world." You sit on the star-slide and let yourself drop down, down, down, back into your waking life.

Monarch of the Luna Glen

You find yourself back in the Luna Glen at dusk. There is a faint light from a waning crescent moon and the landscape has turned to autumn. Muted shades of amber and gold will soon be lost to nightfall, but right now you see the brown of faded heather on the hillsides, the russet and gold of turning leaves. The glen is swathed in autumn mist that swirls around, hiding the summits of the mountains. The fog of your breath mingles in with the mist around you.

The air is damp and you set off walking towards the treeline up ahead to seek shelter. Leaves crunch under foot and you kick the autumnal carpet as you go, just as you did as a child. It feels pleasant to tramp through the leaf-fall. It reminds you of all your autumns past, as the year sheds the weight of former glory and prepares for the next stage of growth. You realise that is what you are doing too – shedding old woes and former triumphs, and preparing for new challenges and the personal growth that they bring.

The evening is still, but for the sound of your own footsteps... and then, someone else's. Someone is walking behind you, at a distance, but coming closer. You stop in your tracks and look over your shoulder to see who it is, but no-one is there, nor can you still hear their footsteps. You turn back and continue on your journey. Once again, the footsteps resume behind you, closer this time. Listening carefully, you realise that the sound is different from the one your feet make as you walk. Rather than a gentle trudge, this is a clop, clop, clop, clop, in a steady rhythm, just behind you. Someone, or something, is following in your footsteps. It moves when you move, it stops when you stop.

You look round again, but still you can't see anyone, yet you can feel a presence and it isn't human. You wonder who is following you and, in the spirit of courage, you decide to stand your ground. Turning, you stand in the depths of the glen and call out to your mysterious companion, "I know you're there! I can hear you. Who are you?" There is no reply, so you say "I am a Seeker of the Old Ones. I mean you no harm. Will you show yourself to me?"

There is silence in the misty glen and no-one answers your call. You wait for a few moments, taking in your surroundings as night descends upon the glen and the waning moon offers little light. Still nothing, only silence and the gentle sound of your own breathing. You continue on your walk as the shadows deepen, trudging through the leaves as quietly as you can, listening out for any sound, but all remains still and you imagine your silent companion has found a different path.

All of a sudden you hear a loud bellow and the sound of thunder. No, not thunder... hooves! A wild, rampaging stag comes charging out of the tree line just ahead and gallops full pelt towards you. You stand your ground. You are not afraid, just wonderstruck. He is beautiful! He has a full rack of antlers and you estimate that he carries at least sixteen tines, possibly

more, bearing them proudly upon his head. He gazes at you for a moment, then throws up his chin and bellows again, before lowering his antlers to the ground, using them to toss the autumn leaves around. When next he lifts his head, he has russet leaves, old thistles and bits of grass hanging from his antlers. He looks like a Yuletide tree and you giggle at the sight of such a bold, majestic creature looking so ridiculous!

The stag clip-clops towards you on cloven hooves. As he comes closer, you notice that his fur is pure white, his antlers silver-grey and he gleams, even in the shadows of the night. He is a white hart! You watch in awe as this most magical and enchanted of stags walks towards you, sure-footed in the leaf-fall upon his dainty hooves. He stands a short way in front of you, bellows again and tosses his antlers. He is waiting for something.

Then it dawns upon you that this magical creature with sixteen tines, is the Monarch of the Luna Glen and you are a guest in his realm. You remember your manners and give him a respectful nod, saying, "Merry Meet, White Hart! I am honoured that you should come to welcome me to your beautiful glen." The stag bows his head in acknowledgement and comes closer. Once more, he lowers his head to the ground, but this time he is trying to catch your scent, sniffing up the length of you, from your feet, right up to the hair on your head. Seemingly satisfied that you are harmless, he nuzzles your hair, then blows gently on your face in greeting.

When the stag pushes his nose into your hand, you take this to be an invitation to pet him, so you stroke the velvety fur of his face and muzzle. You are close enough to gaze into the liquid brown of his eyes, to breathe in the earthy scent of him – like mud and moss, berries and leaves. He smells of the autumnal landscape that is his home. You gently scratch the middle of his forehead and he pushes towards you, playfully nuzzling your hair in reciprocation of your grooming fingers.

Next the stag nods towards the floor and somehow, you just know that he is asking you to kneel down. Placing all your trust in him, you kneel before the majestic beast and hold your breath in wonder as he gently rests his chin on your right shoulder, then your left, followed by your right shoulder again. The Monarch of the Luna Glen has just knighted you! You are now a peer of his Moonlit Realm.

As you remain kneeling, the stag places his muzzle to your heart and gently breathes his strength and courage into you. You feel his vibrant magic coursing through your veins and you know that whatever life sends your way, from now on, you will always have the courage of the stag with which to face it. You reach up and put your arms around the White Hart's neck, hugging him in gratitude for the gift he has just given to you. To your great surprise, the stag kneels also and once again, you have a deep knowledge that he is inviting you to climb onto his back.

Carefully, you mount the stag and settle yourself down in the curve of his spine, holding onto the thick white fur of his ruff. In a smooth motion, the stag raises himself up onto his forelegs, then his hind legs push you up high off the ground and he trots off back into the Moonlit Forest. He carries you easily, as if he is used to bearing your weight. You smile in glee at the feeling of riding through the woods on the back of a wild stag, his antlers spread out before you, his hooves churning up the forest floor. When he breaks into a canter you clutch tightly onto his ruff, digging your fingers in even deeper in an effort to keep your seat. Gaining speed, he lifts his chin so that his antlers flatten against his sides, resting by your legs, as the tree trunks speed by in a blur.

This is pure freedom! The ground slips by beneath you and the branches catch at your clothes. The dancing silver hooves beat out the rhythm of the forest and you are exhilarated by it. This is like flying! You laugh in joy at the wonder and speed of it all, as the stag gallops along full tilt, carrying you through the Moonlit Forest. He is nimble and swift, dodging tree roots and overhanging branches with perfect ease. He is showing you what he can do, what it means to be a stag and run free with the deer herd. He is proving that you will always be safe in his care, no danger could possibly catch up with you when he spirits you away like this. He is allowing you to experience the kind of strength and speed that you could never achieve on your own two feet. He snorts as he gallops, his breath and yours mingling in the night air, becoming one together as you ride swiftly through the shadows and ribbons of mist.

Weaving and turning, dipping and ducking, the stag carries you further into the deepest part of the forest, nipping in and out of the halls of trees as if they are not even there. The two of you make a ghostly sight, the White Hart and his astral rider, flashing by in a streak of silver and white, his hooves drumming on the forest paths and deer tracks, your gasps of delight the only sounds hanging on the night air.

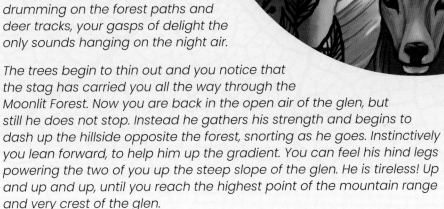

The trees begin to thin out and you notice that the stag has carried you all the way through the Moonlit Forest. Now you are back in the open air of the glen, but still he does not stop. Instead he gathers his strength and begins to dash up the hillside opposite the forest, snorting as he goes. Instinctively you lean forward, to help him up the gradient. You can feel his hind legs powering the two of you up the steep slope of the glen. He is tireless! Up and up and up, until you reach the highest point of the mountain range and very crest of the glen.

Then the White Hart gathers his quarters beneath him and makes a mighty leap into the unknown, into the void on the other side of the mountain and you feel yourself catapulted forward... into the nothingness of air. The magic White Hart vaporises underneath you, turning into silver mist and you are left floating gently down, down, down, back into your wuking self.

Midnight Hare

You arrive in the Moonlit Forest at the stroke of midnight. The witching hour is here and anything can happen! You feel a sense of excitement and anticipation as you begin to walk along the forest path. The moon is almost full tonight and the silver light filters through the tree canopy and dances on the carpet of bluebells around you. You breathe in their heady fragrance and watch as they nod their heads in the night breeze as you pass. It is almost as if they are bowing down to you in greeting. Then you notice something that makes you stop in your tracks.

Up ahead, in the middle of the path sits a hare, her grey-brown fur silvered in the moonlight, her face turned up towards the sky. She sits in perfect stillness, gazing lovingly up at the moon. It seems as though she has been hypnotized. She is mesmerized by the moon. You are mesmerized by her. Her long ears are folded along the curve of her back and her nose twitches slightly as she sniffs the night air. You wonder if the moon has a scent that only she can smell. All of a sudden her trance is broken and she becomes aware of your presence. In a flash she is off, dashing through the forest her bob-tail flashing white in the moonlight.

You take off after her, struggling to keep up because she's so fast! Her hind legs power her forward in great leaps and bounds as she makes her way to a clearing in the forest. You chase on, stumbling over tree roots as you go, but you know that you will never catch her. In the middle of the woodland grove is a large ring of red and white toadstools. You recognize the faerie ring just as the hare

leaps into it and promptly disappears! Without hesitation you leap into the faerie ring after her, experiencing a swooping sensation and darkness, before thumping to the ground in a heap.

Looking around, you witness the hare transforming into a pretty faerie. She is small and dainty, with rosebud lips and large brown eyes. Her ginger hair is curly and wild, falling in spirals to her chin. The skirt of her dress is made from white petals and she wears the trumpet of a white flower on her head as a hat. You blink in fascination, for you've come to realise that you are in the presence of a shapeshifting faerie, not a real hare at all. "Merry meet, Fey One. I am a Seeker of the Old Ones and I apologise if I startled you in the woods."

"You didn't startle me," the faerie reassures you. "Welcome to Elphame, Seeker of the Old Ones. This is the land of the faeries. I am Moonflower. Look for me in the moonbeams bright, feel my magic only at midnight. I have been waiting for you, so that I could show you something. Come with me."

The faerie flies ahead, fluttering on silver gossamer wings. You follow in her wake, walking through a forest similar to the one in your own world, but here the bluebells tinkle like real bells in the breeze, and you can see lots of tiny eyes peering at you from the foliage. Moonflower leads you towards an old well, set in the middle of a crossroads in the forest. The well bears a sign that says **Well of Inspiration – Drink and Know Thy Destiny!** There is a golden chain, from which hangs a matching ladle.

"Will you drink from the golden cup, Seeker, and discover what kind of inspired action will lead you to your destiny?" Moonflower asks, perching herself neatly on the wall of the well.

"I will!" you say, as you turn the handle of the well. The golden ladle begins its descent into the darkness. It takes a long time until you hear a faint splash, then you start to draw the ladle back up again. When it reaches the top of the well, you reach forward and pull the ladle toward you. It is full to the brim with a pale, frothy amber liquid. "Drink, Seeker, and allow yourself to be inspired in the nights and dreams to come," says Moonflower, encouragingly. You take a sip from the ladle and taste a myriad of flavours at once – spearmint, vanilla, sugared almond, wild cherry and more, all rolled into one. It's delicious and you eagerly drink the whole ladleful. All at once you hear music that you hadn't noticed before.

"What is that music? Where does it come from?" you ask.

"Oh that's just the goblin market. They can be a bit rowdy sometimes. Come, I'll show you." Moonflower flies up into the air and you hurry to keep up with her, until you come to a vibrant market town. Looking around you see all manner of fey folk from goblins and elves, to pixies, faeries and brownies. Some are calling out their wares from behind colourful stalls, some seem to be casting magic spells, others are browsing or bartering. You make your way through the crowded market place, entranced and enchanted with the charm of it all.

At the far end of the market you notice a brightly coloured Maypole, bathed in moonlight, with ribbons twining and fluttering as a group of faeries dance around it. As you get closer, Moonflower grabs your hand and drags you towards the pole. "Dance with me, Seeker! Let your worries go and join in the Faerie Revels!" She places a coloured ribbon in your hand and before you know it you are part of the dance, circling round the Midnight Maypole, weaving your ribbon as you dance in and out with your fey companions. The circle dance grows faster and you run to keep up, laughing and enjoying yourself. You feel alive and vibrant, youthful and carefree. This joyful fey magic is good for you. The dancers circle round and round, faster and faster and faster, taking you with them, until suddenly your ribbon snaps off the Midnight Maypole and you spin wildly away from the dance, away from the market and out of Elphame, floating down, down, down, back into your waking self.

Sparkling Swan

You are standing on the edge of a loch. The full moon is shining down, her silvery beams reflecting on the water in dancing light. It is a misty evening and the mist rolls over the loch in smoky clouds. You can smell the pine of the surrounding trees and see your breath in the chilly night air. As you gaze over the water, a beautiful swan glides out of the mist. In the moonlight he looks ethereal and ghostly, a phantom bird gliding upon his enchanted loch. His progress across the water seems effortless, but you know that he is working hard beneath the surface, his feet paddling away, powering him forward, steering him in the direction he wants to go.

He is regal and poised, holding his power quietly inside himself. For all the swan's beauty, they are not flashy birds and you appreciate the quiet confidence that the swan exudes. You wish that you could be more like him. You want to drink in his grace and charm, his strength and power. To you, it seems that he is a Swan Prince, quietly patrolling his watery home, graceful, even as he watches for predators and those who would trespass upon his magical realm.

As the swan moves smoothly across the moonlit water, you track his progress from the shore, walking along the waters' edge to keep up with him. Then, you come upon a silver boat that has been intricately carved, so that the prow is a swan's head and the sides of the boat have been made to look like folded wings. It bobs gently upon the surface of the loch, moored with a golden cord. Laid within it are a pair of golden oars and round about the prow is written the words **Swan Blessed**.

Eagerly you untie the boat, push it further into the loch and jump in. Picking up the golden oars you make your way steadily towards the centre of the loch, where the mystical Swan Prince seems to await you. The water feels heavy as you row, but you push the oars against its resistance and power the swan boat out into the deeper water. Once in the middle of the loch you rest on the oars and look around for the Swan Prince saying, "Merry Meet, Swan Prince. I am a Seeker of the Old Ones. Will you come closer?"

With a ruffle of feathers and a shake of his tail he glides forward, then lowers his head and half opens his wings in a courtly bow, which you return with a nod of the head. As the swan gets closer to the boat, he swims directly over the oar and you begin to pull it in, but notice that he is playfully enjoying the movement of the water which the oar creates. You move the oar in a large circle, under the paddling feet of the swan, then out and over his head. He shakes the water droplets from his head and waits for the oar to come underneath him once more. It is almost as if he is skipping in the water, using the oar as a child would use a skipping rope. His sense of fun and frolicking makes you giggle and you continue this game for a while.

With a trumpeting sound, the swan tucks his head under his wing and begins to nibble at his plumage. You imagine that he is simply grooming himself, until moments later he reappears with one of his purest, whitest feathers in his beak. Stretching out his long, slender neck, he gently drops the feather in your lap. It is a gift from the Swan Prince and you tuck it into your pocket with gratitude. "Thank you, Swan Prince. I will keep it forever, close to my heart and every time I see it, I will remember our meeting and think fondly of you, here on the loch."

Another trumpeting call sounds in the distance and, with a glance over your shoulder, you see a second swan gliding out of the mist. The Swan Prince has a mate! She meanders across the water and you wish her a good evening as soon as she comes close. Then, the Swan Prince dips his head into the boat and tugs out the golden cord, used for mooring. He holds it in his beak, and his mate does likewise. Both swans then begin to pull the boat across the water, into the mist. You stow away the oars and enjoy the ride, thinking how pleasant it is to be pulled along by two kindly, magnificent birds such as these.

As the mist envelops you, it is difficult to see where the swans are taking you, but you have a deep trust that they will guard, guide and protect you. For now, you lay back in the boat, gazing up at the moon and thanking your lucky stars that such magical creatures seem to know that they can trust you too. You drift off into a slumber, as the boat rocks you to sleep.

A little while later, the swans start to make low trumpeting sounds and you awaken, feeling rested and refreshed. Sitting up, you notice that they have pulled the boat towards a small island, hidden in the middle of the misty loch. Then, to your great surprise, as the swan's feet touch land, they transform into people! The Swan Prince becomes a tall, muscular warrior in Celtic dress, while his mate becomes a beautiful woman, dressed in a golden gown of rich velvet. You stare in wonder and they smile at you mischievously.

"Don't be alarmed," says the tall man, formerly the Swan Prince. "I am Aenghus, Lord of Love and this is my wife, Caer. You are most welcome here on Cygnet Isle, Seeker. Anytime you yearn for the peace of my loch, simply blow three times upon the feather from my wing and you will be back in my realm. But now, let us feast!" Aenghus leads the way further onto the island, where there is a round table set with many dishes of fine food. The table and matching chairs are made from twigs and the whole thing has the appearance of an elaborate nest. You feast with the Celtic god and goddess of love and purity, enjoying their company and protection. If you have questions regarding your own love life, now is the time to ask them and allow their guidance to come to you.

Once the feast is over, Aenghus rises to his feet, raises his goblet and says, "A toast to love and to all that are open to it! It is a difficult journey for most of us at times, a tragic one for others and a lonely path until it be found, but it is the meaning of life. To find a soul to mate for life with, heart to heart and spirit to spirit... that is a journey worth embarking upon. To Love!" You raise your goblet and repeat the toast, smiling with enthusiasm. Gently, you stroke the feather in your pocket – Aenghus's promise that he will always be there to love, guide and protect you, and you know that he will guide you to your true soulmate if you are brave enough to follow his lead.

"I have a gift for you too, Seeker," says Caer, shyly. "Here is a Pearl of Wisdom that will guide you to make the right choice in a mate, and in other dilemmas too. As my husband says, the path is never easy, but this pearl will help you to find your true soulmate and Anam Cara – your soul friend. It will help you to make brave and bold decisions." With these words, Caer drops a creamy, iridescent pearl into your hand. You hug her in thanks and place the pearl carefully in your pocket beside the swan feather.

"And now, Seeker of the Old Ones, it is time for you to return to your own realm. Know that you can come back here whenever you need to and, in the meantime, look for me in the swans on the water and in every white feather that you find, for that is my way of letting you know that I am watching over you. Always. Now, climb upon my back and I will take you home."

You clamber onto the piggy-back that Aenghus offers and, as soon as he feels your weight, he begins to run along the shore of the island, turning swiftly back into the mighty Swan Prince. With a leap, he ascends into the air, his mighty wings outstretched, with you on his back and you look down to see Caer, his wife, waving to you and smiling as you leave. You dig your fingers into the soft white feathers of Aengus's slender neck and blow a kiss to the full moon as you pass her by. Then suddenly, the Swan Prince is swooping in a thrilling dive through the sky and you feel yourself dropping down, down, down, back into your waking self.

Lover's Moon

You find yourself standing on a sandy beach, silvered in the light of the full moon, which sails high in the sky, illuminating the ocean below. You are feeling lonely tonight, wondering where your life partner is and what you might do to bring them closer to you. Lost in thought you walk through the shallows of the water, allowing the warm waves of a summer ocean to wash over your feet. It is grounding and relaxing and you begin to feel more content.

You pick up a stick and write your name in the sand, along with the dearest wish of your heart. This wish will remain in place until the tide carries it away to the universe, and at some point it will be returned to you in reality. You feel the truth of this deep down, but sometimes it can be hard to trust that all good things are coming to you, especially when it comes to romance. You've had your fair share of ups and downs, and it can be frustrating at times. Still, you know that there is someone you are meant to be with. All you need is a sign that they are coming to you, that you won't be apart forever and that you will find one another.

You sit on the beach and gaze out over the water. The sounds of the waves gently lapping into shore soothes your troubled spirits and you relax. You notice that the moonlight creates a shimmering path across the water, from the full moon on the horizon, all the way in to shore. You wish that you could walk on water to see where the path leads, but as you stare at the Moon Path, you notice that there is a figure standing on the horizon, silhouetted by the moon.

The figure begins to walk towards you, following the Moon Path of light across the ocean and suddenly you know that this is the soul of the person you are meant to be with. You stand to greet them and wait for them to make their way to you. They walk steadily along the path, not rushing, but coming to you at their own pace. This steady progress reminds you that all things unfold in their own time, not yours. Patience is required, especially in matters of love and the merging of twin souls, but here is a lover who would cross oceans to be with you.

As the figure walks in to shore, you notice they are still shadowy and indistinct. You cannot see their features, there is nothing to help you recognize them in life. They are simply a soul that is meant to connect with your soul. You hold your hands open in welcome and they step onto the sand and take your hands in theirs, then they pull you into an embrace. You feel your heart flood with a myriad of emotions – safety, compassion, trust, acceptance, loyalty, desire, support, attraction, comfort, affection, admiration, respect, humour, protection, consideration, care – this is what love is meant to feel like. This is how you will know that you are in the presence of a soulmate or soul friend.

"I've waited so long for you," you say. "I'm still waiting for you."

"I am coming. Don't give up on us. We are meant to be, and I will find you, I promise."

"But when? I've waited and waited, and you're still not here!"

"I am here now, my love, and I am forever in your heart, as you are in mine. Dance with me, let us enjoy this time and space, while we can." And there, beneath the light of the full moon, with the sound of the waves coming into shore, you waltz with your soulmate, feeling truly happy, and deeply loved, for perhaps the first time. You feel their energy mingling with yours, their soul twinning with yours, the recognition that this is something extra special, a love like no other you have experienced before.

The dance swirls you both around and around, as you move to the combined beat of your two hearts. You are smiling and laughing with your lover, enjoying being in their company, feeling safe and protected. Feeling loved and loving, an equal exchange of affection and respect. When you stop dancing, you walk along the beach, hand in hand. There is no need for words between you, because you know how each other feels and the silence is one of contentment and trust. Suddenly, your lover bends to the ground, picks up a pebble and gives it to you. It is a perfect heart-shape. "Hold on to this until I find you, my love. This is my promise to you, that I will do whatever it takes to reach you."

You take the pebble from your lover and say, "And I will do whatever it takes to accept you and trust you when you come into my life."

"And so our soul-pledge is made. Look for me in the light of the moon on the ocean, see me in the love hearts that fill your world and know that I am coming to you."

"But how will I recognize you?" you ask, fearful again that love might pass you by and leave you lonely forevermore.

"You will know me by the way that you feel in your heart. Look for the one with... and know that it is me." Your lover gives you a clear sign to watch out for, some way to recognize them in the real world. This is just between the two of you, a secret sign that indicates when you are in the presence of your Anam Cara or soulmate.

Your lover then picks up a stick and when you look down, you see your own name written in the sand, and your lover writes their initial beneath it, then encircles both names in a love heart.

"Fear not. Our love is sealed in the sands of time and now, my love, it is time for me to go and for you to return to your own realm. Know that if ever you feel lonely, I am right here on the Moon Path and you can meet me here, whenever you want, until I find you."

Gently your lover takes your face in their hands and kisses you sweetly on the lips, in a promise of things to come. Then they turn and walk back out on to the Moon Path, walking across the ocean. You know that you must let them go, in order for them to find you in reality. You hold tightly to the pebble and the promise it represents, as the sand beneath your feet starts to give way and you are gently sinking down, down, down, back into your waking self.

Soldier's Moon

You find yourself back in the Moonlit Forest and the light of the full moon filters through the trees. You are stumbling along, pushing through dense undergrowth and feeling branches swiping at your face, catching at your hair. You feel exhausted, as if you are in the midst of something that is bigger than you are able to cope with. You stand for a moment catching your breath and you realise that you are hopelessly lost and alone. You don't know which way to turn or which path to take. Despite the moon, everything feels dark and foreboding. All you see is darkness and black shadows in the night.

In a panic you stumble blindly ahead, the twigs cracking beneath your feet. Worry dogs at your heels. However hard you try you cannot outrun it. You wonder when you lost control, when things began to go wrong for you and an image comes to mind, suggesting that, deep down, you already know the exact point at which you took a wrong turn, or the circumstances that brought difficulty into your life. A turn that has led you here, to this moment in time, when you are struggling to see the forest for the trees. Try as you might you can't seem to fight your way ahead. You feel like giving up, giving in and just letting the forest take you, allowing the ivy and brambles to bury you in their strangling grip.

Then someone grabs you from behind. You struggle but to no avail, for the arms that encircle you are strong. Your captor whispers in your ear, "Shhhh! It's okay. I'm on your side. I'm going to let you go, but don't run – this place is a minefield. Understand?" You nod your head and the arms that hold you loosen, allowing you to shake yourself free and you turn to face your captor.

Before you, stands a soldier wearing full camouflage gear, bits of leaves and brambles sticking out of his helmet, his face painted in shades of green and grey and black, so that he blends into the shadows of the forest. On his jacket he wears a badge that you instantly recognize as an ally. He is telling the truth. He is on your side and you can trust him with your life.

For the first time in a long time, you relax and breathe a sigh of relief. You no longer feel alone. Now you have back-up. Strong back-up that can help you through the current situation. You see that the soldier is watching you, assessing you, to determine how much fight remains in you. "Okay?" he asks in a whisper. You nod and he replies, "Right then, let's crack on. Put your hand on my shoulder, or tuck it into my belt and follow me." You do as he says and follow in his footsteps. He seems to know exactly where

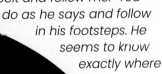

to go and in moments, he has led you deeper into the undergrowth and motioned to you to crouch down, where you are both hidden from view. For the first time, he smiles at you and says, "Sometimes, Seeker, you just have to wait it out for a bit. Give yourself a moment to think and breathe. Just breathe."

You take a couple of deep breaths and feel your nerves begin to steady. His eyes remain fixed on you. He's completely unafraid by his environment. Then he asks you a question, "What's your mission? What brings you here?" and you find yourself telling him about the issues that you are facing right now.

"I just don't know which way to turn," you admit, "I don't know how to get through this. It all feels like it's too much."

"Don't worry, I'll get you to the next checkpoint and you'll receive your next detail of command there. I know it's tricky, but you can do this. I know it's scary, but you're strong and brave. You might feel alone, but you have back-up, you just have to look for it in the right places. All soldiers feel alone from time to time, but we're part of a bigger team and we work together to complete whatever mission we've been given and to achieve the best results. That's what you're doing right now. You're working on the mission and exploring options."

"But I just don't know what to do! How do I get out of this situation? What's the point of it all?" you ask him, to which he replies, "You don't need to see the bigger picture, Seeker. You don't need to know how your whole life plays out. All you need to see is where the next safe step is. All you need to do, is take one safe step after another, one foot in front of the other, and that's enough to get you across any minefield. Are you ready for the next step?" You nod your head and the soldier says, "Right then, let's navigate this minefield. Stay behind me and I'll guide you safely through to the other side."

As before, you follow in the soldier's footsteps, your fingers tucked into his belt, trusting him to lead you in the right direction and get you to a safe place. His presence is very reassuring. It takes time, and progress is slow, but this gives you a chance to mentally work through the issue at hand. You tread carefully, taking the soldier's advice and putting one foot in front of the other. In time you exit the woods and come to a hidden sentry point at the edge of an open field. Another soldier is waiting for you there and your solider introduces you and says "The Seeker has come for their next detail of command."

"Ah yes," says the sentry soldier, "I have it here." He hands you an envelope, which you open and take out the sheet of paper it contains. On the paper is written a clear instruction of what you need to do next, or where you need to look for support. You put the note into your pocket. This is your next command from the universe and the guidance that you seek.

Suddenly you hear the sound of an aircraft and looking up you see a helicopter approaching through the night sky. "Taxi's here!" laughs your solider. "Right, Seeker, this is where I leave you. Take your command and follow it to the letter. When you need further instructions, you know where to find me. Good luck with your mission and stay safe!" He grasps onto your forearm in a soldier's handshake and then he turns and makes his way back across the minefield and into the forest.

The sentry soldier leads you out toward the helicopter and helps you into a backpack of some kind. You climb into the helicopter and thank the pilot for taking you to safety. "Don't thank me yet, you might not like the way home!" he laughs. Puzzled, you settle back in your seat and watch the Moonlit Forest disappear below you. An airman sits beside you, but he is busy looking over the terrain. All of a sudden, he turns to you and says, "Get up, it's time." You get up and without another word, he pushes you right out of the helicopter into mid-air! The backpack jerks behind you and with relief you realise it's a parachute that opens automatically. The canopy opens up above you and you float gently down, down, down, back into your waking self.

Conclusion

Step into The Living Light

The Path of natural magic is filled with living light. It sparkles in the dewdrops on cobwebs, in the sunshine on dancing leaves and in the glimmer of moss, stretching out like a shimmering green carpet before you. It welcomes you into the forest with the heraldic call of a crow, the squirrels guiding your steps as they leap from branch to branch and tree to tree, escorting you along the mystic trail. It beckons from the brook and sings through the trees, as the bluebells bow their heads in reverence as you pass by. It is an enchanting practice, one that brings you closer to nature and the world at large.

I hope that you have enjoyed our little foray into the enchanted forest together and that you have found information and practices in this book to both inspire and empower you. While natural magic can be hard work at times, particularly in the garden, and it carries a certain weight of environmental responsibility, it is a very life-affirming practice that honours the Earth Mother, Moon Maiden, and the Green Man. It is certainly the magical path for the fey-hearted, so let your roots dig deep and your boughs stretch high, as you become the forest-green witch you were meant to be! Farewell my fey-hearted friend, until our next merry meeting.

Serene Blessings,

Marie Bruce x

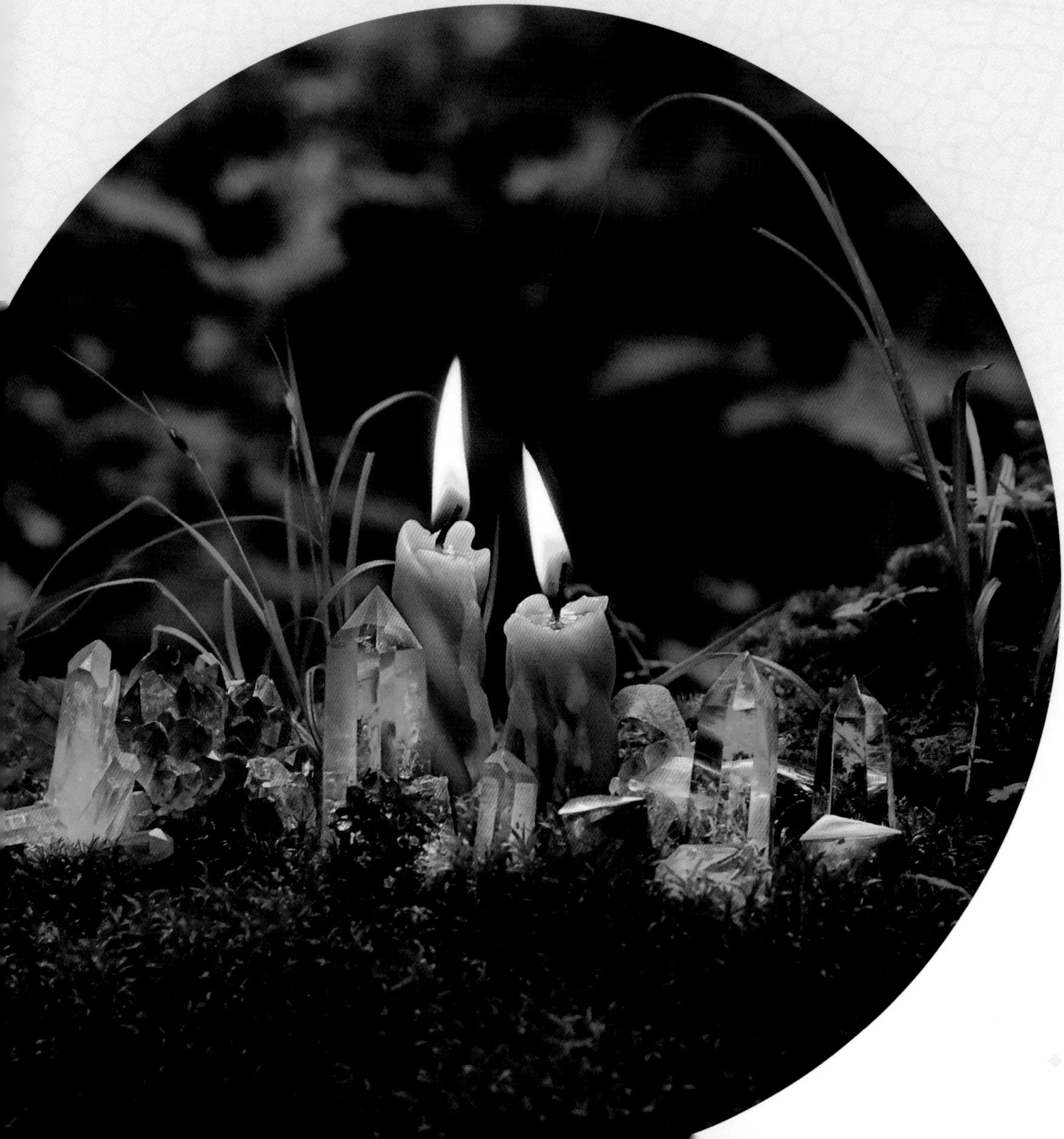

Further Reading

BAILEY, Nick (2015). *365 Days of Colour in Your Garden.* Oxford, Baker and Taylor

CHAINEY, Dee Dee & **Winsham** Willow (2021). *Treasury of Folklore Woodlands & Forests.* London, Pavilion Books Company Ltd

GREEN, Marian (2001). *Natural Witchcraft.* London, Thorsons Harper Collins

HOLLIS, Sarah (1990). *The Country Diary Herbal.* Devon, Webb & Bower Publishers Ltd

INKWRIGHT, Fez (2021). *Botanical Curses and Poisons.* UK, Liminal 11

KINDRED, Glennie (2004). *Earth Wisdom.* London, Hay House

LAWRENCE, Sandra (2020). *Witch's Garden.* London, Welbeck Publishing

MOURA, Ann (1996). *Green Witchcraft.* USA, Llewellyn Publications

MOURA, Ann (1999). *Green Witchcraft II.* USA, Llewellyn Publications

MURPHY-HISCOCK, Arin (2021). *The Green Witch's Garden.* USA Simon & Schuster

PALIN, Poppy (2005). *Craft of the Wild Witch.* USA, Llewellyn Publications

PICKLES, Sheila (1990). *The Language of Flowers.* London, Pavilion Books Ltd

PICKLES, Sheila (1995). *The Language of Wild Flowers.* London, Pavilion Books Ltd

RESTALL-ORR, Emma (2000). *Druid Priestess.* London, Thorsons Harper Collins

Acknowledgments

With extra special thanks to my mother, Jacqueline, for generously sharing with me her green-fingered knowledge, all her gardening books and who used this project as an excuse to buy a few more too! Bookwormery runs in the family! Thanks Mum xxx